GW00570397

Confidence Guru –
Discover a Confident You!

Banish Self-Doubt and Build Lasting Confidence with Proven
Techniques and Strategies from Leading Confidence Coach

Anne Millne-Riley

Edited by Samuel Millne-Ellison and Ian Riley

**Grosvenor House
Publishing Limited**

This book is published by
Grosvenor House Publishing Ltd
Link House
140 The Broadway, Tolworth, Surrey, KT6 7HT.
www.grosvenorhousepublishing.co.uk

A CIP record for this book
is available from the British Library

ISBN 978-1-78623-422-3

This book is dedicated to my wonderful
Aunt Evelyn for all her enthusiastic
support and encouragement of my
endeavours – it has meant so much!

Grateful thanks to Ian, Joe and Sam for your ongoing love, encouragement and support.
Thank you Tina for the cocktails and the inspiration!!

Confidence Guru – Discover a Confident You!

Contents

Introduction

As a professional Confidence Coach I have enjoyed years of experience working with clients from all walks of life; actors, professional sportspeople, company directors, prison officers, dinner ladies, and salespeople. They all wanted to build and develop their confidence so that they could live the lives they wanted to live and be the people they wanted to be – *their true inner self.* I love my work, partly because having originally begun my career in a completely different field, (in the world of advertising) I eventually found <u>my</u> true calling… my true congruent self, and now live my life doing what I enjoy.

The journey to where I am now has taken many years, and I wish I had learnt everything I know now a great deal sooner! However, working with others in this way has been very rewarding. It is such a privilege to work with someone who is struggling to enjoy being themself, to then watch them blossom, becoming truly confident over the following weeks.

I decided to write this book to further the work I do regularly with my clients and to share the strategies and experiences of others. Through their experiences you can begin to change the way *you* feel about yourself and your abilities right NOW. If you can invest a little time and effort into developing yourself through the pages of this book, it will be worth every moment of your time and energy. Imagine working towards the career or lifestyle of your dreams and knowing that you *can* achieve it?

We can *all* be confident… ***But there is a catch!*** You may have read books and articles in the past that have been helpful and given useful tips or insights into how self-confidence can be achieved. You may have found some of these helpful in one way or another, but here we are… you and I… still with work to do on the subject. Am I right?

Here is the catch: To improve confidence we *must* take actions and stretch ourselves at times. However, you will be surprised how quickly self-confidence can be developed as long as you take that leap of faith and actively work on the confidence building strategies in these pages. This book is designed to coach you to self-confidence and coaching itself is a very proactive process.

Now don't panic! Taking action can be painless and gradual, and you will never have to do more than you feel able to do. We will be taking small steps, I promise! I will touch on procrastination and motivation in chapter three, but essentially the reason many of us lack confidence is that we never take any meaningful action towards building that confidence and resilience. Taking action and working through the exercises given in this book will help you to recognise your inner resilience, your inner confidence and will help you to discover or reclaim that unique and wonderful YOU.

It may interest you to know that (like the majority of people) I have not always been so self-confident myself. I came from modest beginnings and sometimes struggled through childhood without the support and encouragement many take for granted. I had to become independent and worried about keeping a roof over my head at a young age. However, I brought myself up in many ways determined not to miss out on the things that other young people might enjoy. I was the first person in my immediate family to attend university and built my own business, partly whilst being a single mother. I am aware that despite my less than salubrious start I was extremely fortunate compared to some of the clients that I have met during the course of my career as a therapist and coach and yet all found the strength and fortitude to become their confident self. My point is that confidence can be achieved by anyone, regardless of their background or upbringing. My confidence came about by developing skills and strategies which helped me to enjoy being me and I have shared my change programme with thousands of others. This book contains these very strategies so that you can find confidence too!

All case studies in this book have been written to protect client's identities and all names have been changed.

Chapter One

What is Confidence?

As a Confidence Coach with many years of experience, I am asked to work with clients regularly who wish to improve their confidence or self-esteem. I have learnt that confidence means different things to different people and so it is always important at the beginning of this work to define what the term *'confidence'* actually signifies in the minds of those individuals. Here are some of the common statements I hear every week.

"To be able to get on with my life without worrying about what others think of me, my work, or how I look".

"To be able to attend meetings at work and contribute my ideas without the fear that someone will laugh at me or think I'm stupid".

"To feel good about myself, to be able to look in the mirror and like what I see".

"To appear confident and professional in an interview… to speak at my daughter's wedding without going to pieces… to feel less shy in social circles… to be able to chat to women without feeling embarrassed…" and so it goes on. An individual's definition of confidence manifests in so many different ways.

The Oxford Dictionary defines confidence as 'A Positive feeling gained from a belief in your own ability to do things well'[1] and *The Readers Digest Universal Dictionary* describes confidence as 'a feeling of assurance or certainty, especially in oneself and ones' capabilities'[2]. Most of us do not need to be 'the best' but simply want to have the self-assuredness to be 'our true self' and you can achieve this far more easily than you might think.

I have heard it said so many times that we are 'born confident'. We did not sit around worrying whether people liked us or whether we appeared stupid in front of our peers back in nursery school. At four years of age, kicking a football around in the back garden, we may have believed that one day we could be the next David Beckham or singing to music in the bedroom, that we might become the next Adele... so what happens to change that feeling of self-assuredness?

The truth is that we are to some extent a product of our experiences and we learn as we develop that not everyone in the world thinks we are beautiful or clever (like Grandma may have done). This comes as a shock at some point when we are young and eventually we begin to realise that we cannot presume to have equal approval and admiration from everyone we encounter. We begin to question what is the truth of the matter; are we, or are we not great?

We begin to evaluate ourselves and our abilities by comparing ourselves to others. We compare ourselves to those around us who we would most like to emulate: the most popular, the most intelligent, the most attractive (in our perceptions). This invariably can lead to a less positive perception about who we are and what we have to offer. We realise that no matter how many times we can skip with a skipping rope – someone else can always do more. As a child, with a child's evaluative brain, this does not sit well with us. Before we began to consider 'confidence' as a concept, we felt we could be 'the best' 'the most beautiful' or 'the most intelligent'. Whether that was true or not did not seem to matter. We felt it and it had given us a certainty about ourselves and our abilities and so of course, we liked who we were.

I will never forget seeing my son, who is an accomplished athlete, run for the first time at a professional running club. He had never lost a race in his young life, from nursery to primary school sports days, he was always the winner. It was expected by everyone in the school and he was known for it. Then one day after asking to join a local running club, aged six, he ran against other accomplished runners for the first time. He was so excited. I warned him that this was a level playing field and that it was possible that he might not win this time. He came third. As a proud mother, I was very impressed. My son, however was so disappointed that he had not won, that he did not return to the club for some time. He began to say to everyone "I'm no good at running".

However, over a period of a few months his love of running became more important than this setback to his confidence and he re-joined the club with a more objective view of his abilities. Nowadays he does not take a defeat as a 'failure' in the same way. He attempts to learn from those that have a more effective technique and is just as focussed on winning.

We all experience these setbacks as we develop into young adults and they can have an effect on how confident we feel to a greater or lesser degree. Although most of us understand that we cannot be good at everything we often still hanker after the skills of others. This is good, healthy, and it should spur us on to continually improve ourselves and our abilities. However, to feel inhibited by the success or confidence of others is difficult to live with and for those reading this and recognising themselves in this description… I'm writing this for you.

It is important to be clear about what confidence is, but also what it is *not!* Being confident is a positive thing which is about self-assuredness and acceptance of oneself and the ability to put oneself forward amongst others. Confidence <u>is</u> <u>not</u> being boastful or arrogant. A confident person feels relaxed enough to accept their areas for development, to seek help and learn from those around them. Arrogant people feel they are always right and are not interested in learning from others.

Confidence comes from the beliefs we have about ourselves and those around us. So something that might shatter one person's confidence might have little or no effect on another individual. It's all about our perceptions and the meanings we give to our own experiences. Negative experiences from the past can cause what are known as *limiting beliefs*. These are the negative beliefs we develop about ourselves, others and the world in general. These beliefs are often formed in early childhood but can remain with us into adulthood. These beliefs are often inaccurate or lose relevance over time but if left unchallenged can inhibit us throughout the whole of our lives. For example, I have worked with many attractive people who have been bullied throughout their school days due to their distinctive appearance, and still struggle to have confidence in their looks.

Case Study

Carl is a prison officer who came to see me concerning his low self-confidence. Like many of the people I meet, Carl had struggled through school due to *Dyslexia,* which was not formally recognised at the time. Dyslexia is a condition that can affect one's educational development in some (but not all) areas. For some, reading can be more of a challenge than for most, spelling might be an issue and short-term memory can affect others. Every dyslexic person has experienced difficulty to varying degrees and the difficulty can be mild to severe. Most dyslexic people are extremely intelligent, excel in many areas, and make up a high percentage of the entrepreneurs in this country. They have had to learn to be adaptive and creative to overcome obstacles, to use the skills they have developed to make their way in the world. However, having been derided for his handwriting and spelling at school, Carl had left at 16 feeling 'stupid'. *His perception of himself was that as he could not always spell correctly this must mean he **was** stupid.* For Carl, this was what has come to be known as a 'limiting belief' which he has always held about himself. Any decisions he had taken in his life had been influenced by this belief. It had prevented him from writing a book he would love to write about football coaching and from joining the local pub's quiz team.

Carl felt very lucky to be in the prison service having entered it shortly after leaving the army and he believed that if he were ever to leave, he would not be able to find a similarly paid job. Although Carl is a confident officer and an articulate speaker, he had never felt able to apply for promotion at work as he has always been anxious about completing forms and written assessments. Carl's belief about himself was that he could not write in the presence of others in case he spelt something incorrectly. Carl can write proficiently, he can complete forms but had always felt anxious about this in case he made an error and might be 'made to feel stupid'. Carl is an intelligent man and an exceptional prison officer but he found this difficult to believe because of his dyslexia. However, dyslexia is understood far better these days by employers and most assessments make allowances for those with the condition. With some support Carl could have been promoted but his 'limiting beliefs' prevented him from trying.

In contrast, I once attended a training course with an inspirational speaker. He was an enthusiastic communicator and the course was fascinating, partly because of the way it was presented. Interestingly, like Carl, James was dyslexic and could not spell correctly at times. However, his perception of himself was that he was an inspiring trainer, whilst acknowledging that spelling was not his strong point. It didn't really matter to James that spelling could be difficult for him as he was confident in his strengths and chose to focus upon them.

James introduced himself at the beginning of the course giving us a brief history of his life and career stating that he knew he was great at what he did, but he then added 'I'm dyslexic however, so my spelling is awful'. He then asked for a volunteer to be his 'spell checker' for the day (not many hands went up to volunteer, but one did) and it was quite amusing the way they worked together when any board writing was required. James was not inhibited by his dyslexia, he bypassed the problem by placing very little importance upon it and focussed on what he was good at. We all respected him for this. It was an amazing course, I learnt a great deal from James, and we all felt 'inspired' at the end of the day.

This brings to mind for me the great quote:

"Whether you think you can, or think you can't – you are right!"

Henry Ford (Founder of Ford Motor Co. and subsequent billionaire)[3]

James was convinced he could present an interesting and inspiring course despite being dyslexic, and he was right!

So one might conclude that feeling confident is knowing that whatever challenges you face, you can remain calm and tackle them to the best of your ability, knowing that your best is good enough. Tackling challenges calmly, which some might consider to be difficult, inspires respect from others. Confident people still feel challenged but they are comfortable knowing that they do not always have the answers. Confident people still experience fear, but they are aware that they can cope with it. Knowing you can cope means you have less fear about taking risks and challenging yourself. Experiencing the difficulty yet succeeding builds that confidence further.

By the same reasoning avoiding challenging situations or decisions can erode your confidence. How are you to know that you *can* cope and flourish unless you continue to act confidently? If you follow the steps to self-confidence found in the pages of this book, you could leave low self-esteem and poor self-confidence behind and move forward in a positive way, beginning to like that person in the mirror. With self-confidence you can enjoy being you. You will feel able to try new things and meet new people, helping you to grow and develop as a person. You may not be 'the best' at everything, but you *can* be excellent – the best that you can be.

Imagine for a moment how that might feel... To get up in the morning and feel excited about putting forward your new ideas at a sales meeting... Liking the way you look in those new jeans... Arriving at a party with an open mind and looking forward to meeting new people... Waiting to start the race and hoping to achieve a 'personal best' time. To recognise that all of the above have the potential for success and knowing that just doing your best is good enough will help you to enjoy each day more and could transform your life.

Notes

Notes

Notes

Notes

Chapter Two

How Confident Are You?

Goal setting is fundamentally the most important task to complete if you wish to bring about change. Knowing what you want to achieve, how you will be sure when you have achieved it, and what that will look like, is important if you are to achieve self-confidence. We will come back to 'goal setting' in chapter three, but first we shall begin with a little self-analysis to assess your confidence levels, your own criteria for success and to determine why and when your natural confidence deserted you.

Complete the Confidence Guru quiz below to discover in which areas you have, or lack confidence, determine your criteria for success in finding true confidence and to identify your areas for self-improvement.

1.   *You have been invited by your new neighbour to call in for a coffee and a chat. Do you…*

   A. Accept the invitation – you may feel a little nervous at first but you will feel fine once the coffee arrives?
   B. Feel excited about making a new friend and arrive with cake!?
   C. Make an excuse about being busy and avoid chatting over the fence to avoid future invitations?

D. Avoid the potential awkwardness of a coffee break but take the time to chat for a little while before making a polite escape?

2. *You have been asked by your boss to brief the department about a new project you have been working on. Do you...*

   A. Find the prospect of presenting a little frightening but ask a close colleague and friend to work with you for moral support?
   B. Agree enthusiastically and feel confident presenting your project to the group? After all you ARE the expert on this project!
   C. Decide that the thought of presenting is terrifying. To avoid anxiety and sleepless nights you come up with a persuasive argument for avoiding it at all costs?
   D. Find presenting a project to colleagues is easy and quite enjoyable for you. After all you get to show off one of your achievements?

3. *You have decided to attend a weekend self-development workshop and the trainer asks for a volunteer to take part in a demonstration for the group. Do you...*

   A. Look around the room smiling and hoping that someone else will step forward but shyly agree if asked directly?
   B. Raise your hand thinking 'this might be fun'?
   C. Look down at your notebook and avoid eye contact? You couldn't possibly stand there in front of all those people.

D. Feel a little apprehensive but step forward if encouraged? You've been on training courses before and you think this should be fairly easy.

4. *You are on a work outing and one of your colleagues asks you to join the Karaoke list to sing later in the evening. Do you...*

A. Agree to take part but then feel anxious all evening?

B. Look forward to your turn and sing enthusiastically?

C. Either refuse, feign a sore throat or leave early to avoid embarrassment?

D. Feel slightly uncomfortable but decide you'll give it a go? Standing up in front of your staff and colleagues is nothing new to you.

5. *The chance arises for an interview for a new job that you feel you could probably do with some support and training. Do you think...*

A. I hope they cannot detect my lack of confidence during the interview?

B. I know I could do this job – I will show them what I'm made of in the interview!?

C. There's no point applying for this job there will certainly be better candidates than me?

D. I feel confident I can get this job, I can do some research and give them what is required?

6. *An impressive 'thank you' gift arrives at the reception desk where you work. Do you think...*

A. That probably won't be for me?

B. Oh that's lovely... it might be for me?

    C. I bet that gift is for Michael, he's such a show off!?

    D. Oh interesting… could that be for me?

7. *You are single and would like to be in a relationship. A nice man/woman you know asks you if you have seen the latest film and if you might like to see it this weekend? Do you…*

    A. Feel surprised, but agree?

    B. Feel excited, and make arrangements?

    C. Feel embarrassed and tell them you are busy this weekend (even though you are not)?

    D. Agree to meet, but feel nervous about how you should dress and how it will go?

8. *Your boss asks if you might like to step up as a supervisor/team leader for three months. Do you…*

    A. Agree as you know it is an opportunity for self-development? However you do worry about how this will be received by colleagues?

    B. Feel delighted and agree? It's great that your potential has been recognised in this way.

    C. Flatly refuse as you feel you would be unable to cope with the pressure?

    D. Think it is a natural next step in your career and accept the challenge confidently?

9. *A friend has asked you to be the Best Man or Matron of Honour at their wedding. However, you are aware that you are their second choice as their best friend will be abroad on that date. Do you…*

    A. Say Yes? After all it is nice to be asked.

    B. Say Yes? You feel very happy to be considered one of their best friends.

C. Say No and make your excuses? You might feel resentful or embarrassed that you are not their first choice and don't favour being in the limelight anyway.

D. Say Yes then proceed to research the role and what is required to ensure you make the best possible Matron/Best Man on the day?

10. *You have an interview tomorrow for the perfect job. Have you...*

A. Worried about this since you applied but have done all the work you can to prepare? You may struggle to sleep tonight?

B. Looked forward to the interview? You have high hopes that it will go well.

C. Decided that it's probably not worth attending? You do not feel prepared and you probably don't have a chance against the other candidates.

D. Prepared fully and done the research? You feel quietly confident.

11. *You are a native English speaker on a holiday abroad and you need to ask for directions – you have been studying a little of the local language. Do you...*

A. Try out your language skills and try to make yourself understood although you might feel a little embarrassed?

B. Try out your new skills and enjoy communicating in another language?

C. Avoid trying to speak to others unless they understand English? It would be far too embarrassing to try speaking a new language in front of others.

D. Learn a few basics and practise them until you feel more confident, then use these phrases when they are needed?

12. *You discover you really like the latest fashion in jeans/trousers. Do you...*

A. Buy them, but you are more likely to wear them just around family and friends?

B. Buy them and look for any opportunity to show off your new look?

C. Decide not to buy them? You don't feel confident enough to change the way you look as it may draw unwanted attention to yourself.

D. Feel happy with how you dress for work but less confident in dressing to reflect your personality on your days off. You might buy them... but will you wear them?

13. *Whilst standing at the bus stand a young passenger throws a crisp packet on the floor which irritates you. Do you...*

A. Pick it up and put it in the bin yourself when they have gone?

B. Ask them nicely to pick it up and put it in the bin provided?

C. Feel irritated inside but do and say nothing?

D. Feel angry but feel unsure what response you will get if you say something? You probably feel annoyed with yourself that you said and did nothing?

14. *When putting forward an idea at work, you feel undermined by a colleague following a dismissive comment. Do you...*

   A. Feel unsure how to challenge this and feel resentful inside?
   B. Tend to challenge their behaviour? You politely ask them to listen to your idea properly before dismissing it?
   C. Say nothing? You would never voice an idea at work although you probably have lots you could offer?
   D. Deal with this professionally? You feel able to express yourself assertively at work and people tend to listen?

15. *A work colleague brings in their newborn baby and offers the child to you to hold (it begins to cry as they are handed over). Do you...*

   A. Take the baby and do your best to sooth them whilst feeling concerned about what colleagues think of you?
   B. Take the baby willingly and ask what you can do to sooth them, unconcerned about onlookers?
   C. Politely refuse with an excuse and exit the scene as soon as possible to avoid embarrassment?
   D. Politely refuse to avoid potential embarrassment stating you are not good with babies, but remain and show an interest in the interests of workplace harmony?

Results

Mostly A's

You feel comfortable amongst your family and friends and are perhaps the first one to get up and dance at a wedding. You tend not to worry too much about how you are perceived by others in a social setting and feel relaxed in your own skin among others who understand and appreciate you for who you truly are.

However, in a work setting you are unsure of how you are perceived by your peers and realise that you have a 'professional persona' which can be very different from the more 'relaxed' version of you. You sometimes doubt your abilities and can feel out of your depth when you are unable to rely on the love and acceptance of friends and family. In the work setting you sometimes feel you have to prove yourself and can worry that people will discover you are lacking in self-confidence. Feeling confident in one area of your life, yet not in another is fairly common.

You are in a wonderful position to develop this area of your confidence. Sometimes You can draw on the success and support you already have to gently step out of your comfort zone and begin to achieve in other areas too. The confidence building strategies in this book could help you to develop those areas of your life where you lack confidence by building on your strengths so that you can feel comfortable being 'you' in any situation.

Mostly B's

You are mostly a fairly confident person. You are comfortable in your own skin. You are comfortable in the presence of high achievers and this does not intimidate you. You see a challenge, like public speaking or meeting new people as an opportunity for personal growth and you are not hard on yourself if you don't get everything perfectly right.

When you achieve something, you are able to congratulate yourself and you can enjoy each little victory. No one can truly claim to be the most intelligent person in the world or the most successful, but you are able to give yourself a pat on the back and you are happy with what you have achieved so far. You achieve things because you can cope with failure, and always come back fighting.

Well done! Your positive 'can-do' attitude helps you to maintain your confidence and gives you the resilience to cope with life's challenges. Use the strategies in this book to help you to maintain your positive confident outlook.

Mostly C's

You question yourself and your abilities all the time even when others seem to have faith in you. You avoid situations where you might stand out or be noticed and feel embarrassed if you have to speak or perform in front of others. You feel it is better to go unnoticed than to look silly or feel embarrassed.

You fear failure and worry about feeling embarrassed or humiliated and how bad you might feel if this happened.

This prevents you from fulfilling all you could achieve and you often avoid a challenge. You tend not to fully trust others, after all, you have been hurt in the past. Occasionally, you may dislike yourself physically and perhaps feel you lack enough intelligence and ability to achieve as others do. A challenge of any kind feels like a risk – not an exciting prospect.

The strategies in this book could set you on an exciting journey of discovery and help you to understand and banish your limiting beliefs. We <u>all</u> have the ability to be confident. By working towards your confidence objectives you can begin to enjoy an exciting new life, setting new inspiring goals and feeling happy to be your unique self!

Mostly D's

You feel fairly confident at work or in other fields of activity where you have been able to develop yourself and know the basics of how to compete, behave and achieve. In a work setting you feel safe to converse with others. You have earned the respect and credibility over a long period of time and do not worry about what colleagues and customers think of you.

However, when it's time for socialising and having to reveal the *real* you – you can struggle. You may worry whether you will be considered interesting or amusing to talk to. You may struggle to talk about subjects that are unrelated to work or feel uncomfortable cooking for others or dancing at the work party. You are used to excelling in the workplace and so being second best at anything socially amongst your family and friends may not sit comfortably with you. You are no stranger to self-development and can enjoy your success in the workplace. You can draw on the success and support you already have to gently step out of your comfort zone and begin to achieve in other areas too.

Working through this book could help you to develop that personal side of your personality and would help you to understand your limiting beliefs. By building your understanding of how confidence is developed you can begin to enjoy social occasions and feel comfortable in your own skin.

Combined results

If your results are mixed and you have more than five of a particular letter you will notice elements of your personality in the paragraphs above for those letters. Identify the gaps in your confidence from these featured elements.

Where did it all go?

Very often an event from our childhood or adolescence is sighted as the catalyst for losing self-confidence and this forms our *limiting beliefs*.

1. Can you remember a time when you felt embarrassed speaking in public? (clients often tell me about a project they were forced to present at school in front of the whole class. A time when bullies sniggered at the back of the class, their mouth became dry and their hands began to shake).

2. Do you remember a time when someone made you feel silly (i.e. a friend laughed at your new jacket)?

3.   Do you remember a parent or teacher being disappointed by your educational results?

4.   Do you remember coming last in sports days or struggling with a particular subject at school?

5.   Were you ever called names in school for the colour of your hair or some other feature of your physical appearance?

6.   Do you remember someone taking you for granted and not valuing your friendship or assistance?

7.   Do you remember someone not believing you although you told the truth?

8.   Did you feel self-conscious about your appearance or anything else when you were a teenager?

You may recognise experiences similar to these from your past and they may help you to pinpoint when a blow to your self-confidence occurred. Of course, during the huge changes you experience throughout your childhood and adolescence, confidence is fragile as we try to come to terms with the changes happening to our bodies. One might feel vulnerable in our first year at high school or on our first day in a new job. It does not take a great deal to erode self-confidence at this point. Can you remember how these events made you feel at the time? As children we are constantly trying to make sense of how the world works using our young and inexperienced interpretation skills. One bad experience talking in front of our peers in class at school can easily be interpreted at a young age as *'I am terrible at public speaking – it is embarrassing and should be avoided in future'*. However, the truth of the matter is – talking in front of your class is a skill, and we should not be surprised if we don't achieve perfection the first time around.

It is important to recognise that we are all good at some things and bad at others. The fact that this is true of all people – even the talented ones, means that if we work positively with the skills and talents we have, rather than what we *don't have,* this makes positive change possible for all. And as for personal appearance, beauty really IS in the 'eye of the beholder'. Look around at all the beautiful people you notice. What makes them attractive? Very often it is not their hair or figure or muscles! Spend a little time 'people watching', you will find that attractiveness comes often from what is inside the person. A self-confident person reveals their personality and it is often relaxing to be in their company as they are so 'at ease'. They may smile more and because they feel good in themselves they are naturally more attractive. In addition, as they value themselves, they may also invest more time in dressing and grooming thus caring for themselves accordingly.

We should now begin to consider what we are good at, fairly good at and not so good at. Like many of my clients in a first session, our prison officer Carl, had difficulty identifying areas in which he excelled. He felt that he was not intelligent and that he held his role as a prison officer more through luck than his own achievements. This is recognised by therapists as *Imposter Syndrome.* It is the common fear that at some point, someone will realise we are no good at what we do and our privileged position will be lost. Carl felt anxious if asked to write in the presence of someone and would feel panicky if he thought this might be required. On one occasion he was told he would have to run a workshop for prisoners the following day which required writing on a white board and he decided to take sick leave in order to avoid this situation. He has always experienced a fear of failure or embarrassment and places a very high value on the ability to write and spell correctly.

Through discussion, it became apparent that Carl was good at speaking in public. He had many years of experience in the service, had some wonderful stories to tell and advice to impart and people tended to listen attentively when he spoke. Carl was often consulted by other officers and often managers about how to work effectively with prisoners and he was exceptionally good at providing guidance on many issues. He accepted that his spelling and handwriting were not always as proficient as his peers, but he could write and spell to a certain level. Carl was the life and soul of a party and was often on the party invitation list. He was popular amongst family, friends and colleagues. It also transpired that he was a gifted footballer and he coached a local team. Unfortunately, Carl never valued the amazing skills that he possessed but had chosen to focus on those skills which he did not possess.

I remember hearing a story about a young boy at my local primary school which really changed my perception of how we should deal with what we consider to be our weaknesses and differences.

Stephen was nine years old, he enjoyed drawing but was dyslexic and this had been preventing him from progressing in school. His teachers were working with him to develop his writing ability but he was far behind the other students. On one occasion the class were taken to a local farm to learn about farming and the animals there. The children were encouraged to take a few notes as they would be asked to write a piece on what they had seen and learnt that day.

On return to school the children set about consulting their notes and planning to write about their experience. Stephen, of course struggled to do this, he hadn't taken any notes and whilst he waited to speak to the teacher he began to draw some sketches of machinery and animals which he had encountered. When the teacher came to his desk, she was astonished by the quality of his drawings and the fine detail. Stephen had recorded his experiences through his drawings. It became evident where Stephen's talents were and he was encouraged to complete his project using drawings alone. They were later displayed in the school hall and Stephen's mother was asked to attend an assembly where they would be presented to the whole school. Naturally Stephen continued through school in the usual way but the confidence he gained when his drawings were appreciated had a huge impact on his future. Stephen went on to study fine art at university.

His story reminded me of a terrific book that encourages the reader to turn around an otherwise unsuccessful situation to get something positive from it. In Michael Heppell's great book *'Flip It – How to get the best out of everything'*[4] Heppell sets out his simple formula for no longer allowing 'limiting beliefs' to prevent you from succeeding. Whatever life throws up at you, his formula challenges the limitations and finds a positive. It's all about using what you have and not wasting time and energy on what you don't have!

As work progressed with Carl, we began to focus on the unique skills he possessed. Carl held the respect of many, both colleague's and prisoners. He knew this but worried that if he revealed his dyslexia to others, he might lose that respect. We began to explore the possibility of using his experiences of dyslexia in a positive way. We discovered that an extremely high percentage of prisoners suffer from dyslexia. For many, it has been cited as the reason some prisoners had broken the law in the first place. Not feeling able to attend college or fill in application forms had led them to what they felt was an inevitable life of crime. We discovered a list of famous achievers who are said to have also lived with dyslexia – Albert Einstein, Pablo Picasso, Winston Churchill, Henry T. Ford and John Lennon, to name just a few.

Carl took the bold step of volunteering to take part in some of the workshops being offered to prisoners to improve employability skills. Together, we developed a brief talk about how dyslexia had made life difficult for him and how he had felt limited by this, which he delivered during workshops on *positive thinking.* He was able to relate how he had made the most of what he had to make a career and life for himself. The response from prisoners and staff was overwhelming. Prisoners often felt boosted by these talks and could see that despite their limitations, perhaps on release, they could find something to do that they were good at. More surprising for Carl were the number of staff who came forward and confided that they had been battling with dyslexia themselves and felt they understood and were liberated by his story. Carl became far more respected by staff and prisoners following his choice to reveal his 'weakness'. He became a little famous throughout HMP circles and has been asked to talk to a number of schools and other prisons in the area. Today he has been promoted having been encouraged by his manager to take his assessment for promotion and has his sights set on being a Governor at some point in the not too distant future. Naturally, this has made a positive impact on Carl's confidence, he is happy to be him, with all his wonderful strengths and wonderful weaknesses.

Exercise

Spend some time considering your strengths and weaknesses – write EVERYTHING down, no matter how small – it is all relevant. If you are struggling to find your strengths, ask friends or family to help you by giving some suggestions.

_____
_____
_____
_____
_____
_____
_____
_____
_____
_____
_____

Consider the strengths that you and others have noticed in you. How could these be utilised? Being able to write neatly might seem like a useless skill, but to a calligrapher, this would mean *everything*.

So what is it that you wish to achieve? What would confidence mean to you?

You should begin by defining who you are deep down and what you want to share with the world and others around you. Are you happy in your work, studies, or lifestyle and if not, what would you like to spend your life doing? The answers to these questions will form an important part of your goal setting.

Case Study:

Kay, one of my clients, had a dark birthmark just above her right eye. She had so many comments made about this at school that she had tended to grow her hair longer to cover this unique part of her. Kay spent many years wishing the mark was not there. During our work together we defined what self-confidence would mean to Kay. She just wanted to be liked (and loved by someone special) for who she was. She did not want anything to limit her happiness or career. Of course, Kay's birthmark was not a limiting factor but her lack of self-confidence was! The way she felt about it did limit her in all areas of her life as she allowed unhappy memories and comments from her past to damage her self-confidence. As part of our goal setting we began to write together a *'confident me'* statement to focus our work upon. This was to be a visionary statement that would inspire Kay and which would define how Kay wanted to be perceived by others in the future. It provided a focus and criteria for success. And here it is…

'I am Kay. I am an attractive and outgoing person. I like to talk to people and enjoy socialising. I am working hard to develop my career and want to start my own company one day. I like dressing up and socialising and I am happy to be me.' (this is who Kay truly was inside – her lack of self-confidence was the only thing that was preventing her from being her true self in everyday life).

We began to consider the options. If Kay felt strongly about her birthmark, perhaps there was some cosmetic procedure that could disguise it. Personally, I felt the mark was really not an issue and believed it did not impact on her attractiveness. I believed it was a unique part of her and that it should remain. Thankfully, Kay felt just the same. Through our sessions Kay took the decision to have her hair cut in a style she really loved, which would reveal her birthmark, something she had avoided for most of her life. She took this bold step in order to explore whether this was something she could live with in the future. The next time I saw Kay, she looked great! Her hair was amazing, she had decided she would try colouring it and so she looked very different. Kay had had so many positive comments from friends and co-workers about her new look, you could see she was already becoming more confident. That day, the birthmark was never mentioned, not once. Kay was now so focussed on other things she wanted to achieve, it seemed to have slipped her mind. She mentioned some weeks later that her nephew had drawn attention to it on one occasion, "What is that on your head?" Kay laughed, "I told him that it is my birthmark and that when I see it in the mirror, it reminds me of how unique I am!"

As time went on Kay related that she rarely noticed the mark when she looked in the mirror. It became irrelevant. Kay began her business far quicker than either of us expected and she became extremely motivated as her confidence grew. She now works alongside her fiancé John (who by the way, thinks her birthmark makes her look unique too!) and they are building a great online business together. Kay has felt more able to socialise and loves the opportunity to 'dress up'. She has a growing social circle and loves going to cocktail bars and restaurants.

Exercise

Write your own 'confident me' statement. If you had self-confidence and felt able to reveal the 'true you', what would people see when they met you? What would you share with the world?

_____
_____
_____
_____
_____
_____
_____
_____
_____
_____

Exercise

Now consider what you would like to achieve in your life. This could relate to any of your dreams or aspirations no matter how large or small. It could relate to your personal life or career.

_____
_____
_____
_____
_____
_____
_____
_____
_____
_____

Exercise

When you have recorded the desired achievements above now write a *success statement* by asking yourself how you will feel when you *are* confident. This is what Kay had stated:

'I will enjoy my life more. I will think more about the ideas I have to improve my team's performance and no longer worry about sharing these thoughts and ideas. I will enjoy getting dressed up for a night out and will make the most of what I have. I will enjoy having my hair shorter. I look forward to progressing in my career and no longer worry about what people think of me. I will feel excited at the prospect of having my own company'.

_____
_____
_____
_____
_____
_____
_____
_____
_____
_____
_____

Now that you have considered how your life could truly change once you have found lasting confidence, let's make a start!

Notes

Notes

Notes

Chapter Three

Setting Goals and Maintaining Motivation

The importance of goal setting has already been discussed but what are *your* confidence goals and how will *you* know when and if you have achieved them?

Do you want to be able to speak up and contribute more in meetings or in social gatherings? Do you want to feel more confident about your appearance? Do you want to have the confidence to flirt? Do you want to be able to join a dance class and feel comfortable chatting to other members?

For a goal to be achieved it must first be *defined*. We need to have a sense of what it is that we want in our lives and also when we want this change to happen. Without a timescale to work to, our goals are likely to drift away from us. In addition, we must also be aware of how our success can be measured.

Case Study:

Mark wants to contribute more in meetings at work. He is always worried about how others value his ideas and this prevents him from speaking in front of his colleagues. His limiting belief has been: *I cannot speak in public, I am no good at it and everyone will think I am stupid if I try*. Mark wrote his 'confident me' statement which read as follows:

*I am Mark, I may not be the best public speaker in the world, however, I have worked hard to develop my skills and prepare for meetings so that I can contribute ideas and ask relevant questions. I am open minded enough to invite feedback, build on areas of weakness and enjoy receiving positive feedback. I **can** and **do** speak in public!*

Mark's goal is to be better at public speaking and to feel more able to contribute ideas amongst his colleagues. Ultimately, the key to achieving this is in finding a structure in which he can begin to build his skills. By defining a goal and criteria for success, he can grow and improve in this area and know when he has achieved what he set out to do.

Mark's *defined goal* is to contribute an opinion, thought or idea in every meeting that he attends each month. He intends to try to improve on his delivery each time and has asked his line manager to give him some confidential constructive feedback on this. Mark has created a deadline to work to, to prepare what he will say at each meeting and how he will present these ideas. Remembering that perfection is rarely required, he plans to use any feedback as an opportunity to improve his communication skills. He has researched methods of controlling his nerves and found a useful breathing technique to help him to prepare for each meeting.

So where does Mark get the 'courage' to take action on what for him has been a difficult task in the past? Mark simply wants to improve his speaking skills and self-confidence. Focussing on this and understanding that mastering these skills are necessary in order to gain promotion, he can gradually take himself out of his comfort zone and work through some key steps managing his anxiety through a number of useful techniques. Motivation is key if we are to change the way we perceive ourselves and to change the negative thinking habits of a lifetime. It is often thought that motivation is required before we can take action, but it in fact happens the other way around. By taking some small action, we move towards our goals and then become more motivated. It is motivation that helps us to work through difficulties and barriers and confidence grows with each small achievement.

Exercise:

Write down one small thing you could do today to move you closer to achieving your goals.

_____

_____

_____

_____

_____

Case Study:

My client Sandra was just 50 years of age when I met her for the first time. Sandra had never worn makeup. She had lost her mother at a young age and had no sisters and so there had never been a role model to help her to learn about how to dress, use makeup and choose perfume. These may seem straightforward and simple skills to someone who possesses them. However, applying makeup for the first time and then being seen in public wearing that makeup can be very daunting for someone with no experience of this. When they look in a mirror they are used to seeing themselves without makeup and sometimes even the smallest amount can look overpowering as it can dramatically change one's appearance.

Sandra would love to wear makeup and admires her friends who wear it every day. She loves the appearance of lipstick especially, but whenever she has tried to apply it in the past she has never known if it looked right and felt silly asking others for advice. She told me…

'I am 50 years of age… I cannot tell anyone that I don't know how to apply makeup!'

This limiting belief had prevented Sandra from being who she has always wanted to be (her true self).

We began our work, discussing Sandra's goals. What did Sandra want to achieve? What did she want to avoid? Sandra wanted to learn the skills and have the confidence to know how she could apply makeup in a way that would flatter her looks. She wanted to experiment with different looks and to find the right one for her. Sandra did not want to draw too much attention to herself. Indeed, it has been her shy nature that had to some extent prevented her from tackling the issue and trying out new things in the past. Sandra has a good circle of friends and socialises fairly regularly but feels uncomfortable with the thought of changing her appearance and the attention this might attract.

After some discussion we were able to write Sandra's *confident me* statement:

I am Sandra, I wear makeup and have taken time to discover my own unique look. Having taken professional advice, I have been able to explore different looks and have found the one that suits me best. I wear makeup each day, especially during evenings out with friends. I feel confident wearing makeup and no longer feel embarrassed.

Step 1: We began by booking Sandra a session with a makeup artist. Sandra cut out magazine photos and took them to the session to show the artist the looks she liked and those looks she wanted to avoid. The artist tried a number of makeup styles with Sandra, showing her the techniques and advising her on the best way to use make up for her age and complexion. Photographs were taken in the session to reflect upon. Sandra came out of the session having learnt the basics of makeup application. She bought a set of makeup and practised each evening after work so that she could get used to seeing herself in the mirror wearing makeup. Having specialist advice helped Sandra to understand what looks suited her best.

Step 2: Sandra's confidence was growing but she was concerned about arriving for a social evening looking so different. Together, Sandra and I organised a 'pamper evening' for friends to raise funds for a local charity. Sandra provided some wine and nibbles and the purpose of the evening was to give each other pedicures or manicures and to pass on tips and general knowledge about how each one applied their makeup. Sandra's niece, a massage therapist was also on hand to give shoulder massages. It was an enjoyable evening and Sandra was able to introduce the 'new her' in front of friends in the safety of her own home. Sandra was also able to learn from the feedback of others and this boosted her confidence further.

Step 3: Sandra's next social engagement was used as the opportunity to leave her home wearing makeup for the first time. She felt fairly confident following the pamper evening and the positive comments she received from friends boosted this further. She told me, "I felt like a different person somehow, sophisticated and feminine."

Now Sandra enjoys trying new lipsticks and eye shadows. She wears makeup most days and enjoys the way it makes her feel.

By following her defined goals through some simple and logical planned steps, Sandra was able to overcome her barriers, taking herself gradually out of her comfort zone. Times and dates were defined and so this was all accomplished in one month. She could hardly believe that something she had struggled with all her life could have been accomplished so quickly.

How to set your confidence goals

I cannot stress enough the importance of goal setting! Having defined goals gives you clarity in your thinking, keeps you motivated, and helps you to work through barriers to achieve success in a timely way.

There have been a few studies regarding the effectiveness of defined long-term goal setting and any qualified coach will tell you that goals are paramount if you are to achieve your aims. Setting meaningful goals helps us to work to an achievable time-frame, take positive actions and prevents us from getting side-tracked. They, above all, help us to focus on what needs to be done (and when) which propels us forward, tackling obstacles efficiently in order to stay on task. Without defined goals, It's like trying to find a destination without using a map, you are almost certainly going to get lost!

Goal setting is SO important and the more defined the goals are – the more success you will have with the changes you wish to make. Goals should be SMART that is:

Specific – Measurable – Attainable – Realistic and Timely[5]

Specific – Unspecific, vague goals often do not motivate the individual to success and you achieve a 'specific' goal far easier as it provides the focus you require to get the job done. A general goal might be to 'lose weight'. But a specific goal would define the desired goal weight, outline a specific plan of action with a deadline date, and would state why you wished to achieve it.

Example:

Your goal is to lose one stone in weight in order to get back into your old clothes and feel more confident and happier about your appearance. You want to achieve this by the 21st of November – your birthday. Therefore, you plan to join a gym and see a personal trainer three times a week. You will also follow a diet regime from a local diet club and attend that diet club each Saturday morning and will weigh-in and heed any advice needed. You will also stop buying bread except at the weekends.

Measurable – To ensure you would reach the weight goal above by the 21st November one would have to consider how much weight you would need to lose each week prior to that date to accomplish the task on time. When the steps required are defined and measured, you can ensure you are on track at each stage and experience the sense of achievement that accompanies each weekly loss and this would motivate you still further to accomplish the final goal. You would set target dates to ensure you are remaining on task; *i.e. lose three pounds by the 1st of September and seven pounds by the 20th of September*. Then, if you reach the 1st of September and you have not lost three pounds, you have a little time before the next weigh-in to decide what must be done and to make swift changes so that you can meet the target of seven pounds on the 20th of September.

Setting goals that are **_Attainable_** is important if you are to succeed. If your goal was to be able to run a marathon in three weeks' time with no previous experience, then you would be unlikely to achieve this. You might become exhausted or injured and feel demotivated. However, if your goal was to run a marathon and achieve a specific time in six months' time, you would have the time to build your strength, stamina and skills and be better placed to achieve this successfully. Setting unattainable goals will only lead to a feeling of demotivation.

As well as being possible to attain, a goal should be **_Relevant_**. Your goal should stretch you and should represent something you really want or need which you are willing to work for. If your goals do not stretch you a little and their outcome provide you with something you really want, then you are unlikely to put the sufficient effort in to achieve it. Equally, to ensure you do not waste valuable time and effort, you need to ensure achieving each goal will give you ultimately what you want.

And finally, goals should be **Timely**, which means there should be a specific time-frame in which to achieve them. Without a deadline to meet there will be no sense of urgency to complete the steps required. The timescale itself must be achievable of course so if I wanted to lose one stone in weight between the 20th August and the 21st November this would be very achievable as I could lose weight at a rate of around one pound per week. However, if I wanted to achieve a weight loss of one stone in half the time it would require more work, and in a quarter of the time, a much more radical approach! The trick is to set a timescale that is not too far away and gives you the motivational challenge.

I believe the one letter missing from this acronym is D for **_Documented_**. When you set a defined and specific goal the plan <u>must</u> be documented so that you can chart your progress. If you are trying to save money for an exciting trip abroad, you could perhaps put your weekly target each week in your diary. Also note in your diary the progress that you make. If you don't have a diary – get one!! A calendar simply won't do and a diary will become part of your daily journey ensuring that you remain on track to your success. Any other visual aids which might help you to chart your progress will be useful. I once drew a pie chart and stuck it on the fridge door when I was raising money for a project. Colouring it in each time I made a deposit at the bank motivated me, it felt like a celebration, and helped me to achieve my goal far quicker than I had expected.

Setting goals are essential if you are to make the changes to your confidence and your life that you wish to make! Begin by using the SMART form overleaf: Think about what you wish to change. Why do you want to change this and by what date? Ask yourself how you will know you have achieved your goal, how will it feel, what will it look like? Use your imagination and don't hold back! You deserve to feel confident in your own skin and to find your true place in the world. Why not write a *confident me* statement like Kay, Mark and Sandra did to help you to focus on the end result you want to achieve?

Begin by completing 'What you want to achieve "specifically" and when'. If you have a number of goals, complete a form for each one. Write and re-write until you are happy that this plan will not need to be altered and you can copy this out and put it somewhere where you can monitor your progress daily/weekly (on the fridge or in the back of your diary). Ask yourself each morning 'what can I do today that will bring me closer to my goal?'

SMART Goal Form

Specific: What do you want to achieve 'specifically' and for when (specific date). What steps will you take to achieve this and how often. State why you wish to achieve this goal - what will the achievement give you?

_____
_____
_____
_____
_____
_____
_____
_____
_____

_____
_____
_____
_____
_____
_____
_____

Measurable: In order to achieve your goal, what steps will you need to take and by when? set a timescale and deadlines to achieve each step.

_____
_____
_____
_____
_____
_____
_____
_____
_____
_____
_____
_____
_____
_____

Attainable: Is the goal possible to achieve? If not, ask yourself what attracted you to this ideal and what else could give you the same rewards?

_____
_____
_____

_____

_____

_____

_____

_____

_____

_____

_____

_____

_____

_____

_____

Realistic: Is your goal ambitious enough and once attained, will it give you the change you are looking for? Don't be afraid of setting a goal that reflects your true dreams and desires, if you don't aim for these specifically, they will never happen!

_____

_____

_____

_____

_____

_____

_____

_____

_____

_____

_____

_____

_____

_____

Timely: Work out the time-frame and the specific actions required that you must complete in order to attain your goal. How and when will you check you are on-track along the way?

_____

_____

_____

_____

_____

_____

_____

_____

_____

_____

_____

_____

_____

_____

_____

_____

Document it!! Once you have completed your smart goals, start putting important actions and deadlines in your diary to ensure you are focussed on them each week and month. Plot your course to success and congratulate yourself when you achieve each step.

10 Tips to keep you motivated

1. Plan actions and place them in your diary, tick them off when you complete them for that feel-good factor.
2. Make a commitment. Whether it is agreeing to take some actions with a confidence coach or promising

your son you will complete an action by Tuesday. Promising someone important that you will tackle something increases the chances of you doing so.

3. Make sure your inner voice helps you along the way. Think of some motivational statements or affirmations that can help to keep you focussed on the reasons why you need to keep going e.g. *getting fitter will help me to live longer for my children, OR If I can complete this essay by Friday, I can celebrate on Saturday.*

4. Keep momentum – It is easier to motivate yourself when you are already succeeding. Motivate yourself daily by setting small goals and remember to tell yourself how well you are doing!

5. Keep healthy – Eat healthily, sleep plenty and get some fresh air. If you are tired and lacking in energy it is difficult to keep motivated.

6. Get support – Get a close friend or family member to support you and help to motivate you by showing an interest in your progress and encouraging you to maintain focus.

7. Make a chart   Whether you are trying to raise funds to buy a house or taking actions to make yourself more employable, draw a chart and colour in each segment as you go along so that you can see your ongoing progress. Having this visual reminder of your goal and your success so far helps to keep you motivated.

8. Allocate time – Make sure you have set aside some time to take the actions you need to take. If you do not allow enough time, you can feel discouraged whereas scheduling some time in your diary will help you to maintain momentum.

9. Sabotage-proof your plan – If you know you may struggle to make a trip to the gym in the morning agree to meet someone there so you are more likely to get up in time.

10. And finally, if you lose momentum and motivation and feel low, draw a line under the progress so far and start afresh tomorrow! Revisit your plan and reschedule actions so that you can get back on track… then have an early night!

Notes

Notes

Notes

Chapter Four

Busting the Barriers to Confidence

As with the case of Carl, sometimes we are less confident than others because of a perceived lack of skill in a particular area. Although many other people are the same and appear to be able to accept this and develop their other skills, for some this forms a barrier to becoming confident. Often we can be confident in some situations and yet still struggle when our weaknesses are challenged. We all have these barriers to some degree and it may surprise you that even the people you believe to have everything, the success stories, the talented and famous, often have doubts about their abilities and still need to work on their confidence.

At the time of writing I have recently read online that a leading American actress is believed to have worked with a confidence coach and a primetime TV celebrity has also shared her difficulties with anxiety and low self-confidence in the media in recent months. I work with actors and celebrities on strategies to help them to cope with low self-confidence so I am aware that this can be a problem for anyone. Being in the public eye can place huge pressures on an individual to maintain the personal and the public profile or persona they wish to portray in order to retain successful careers. So maintaining and enhancing how they are viewed by others is perhaps more important than it would be for many of us. Yet working with this type of client simply serves as a reminder to me that we are all human, with the same challenges, doubts and limiting beliefs.

To realise that absolutely everyone lacks confidence at times is very important. It reminds us that no matter how successful someone is, they are still human and they still experience self-doubt at times. Many of the people I work with believe that everyone in their social circle are confident and that they are the only one to suffer from self-doubt. I worked with a young mother who was too shy to talk to other mothers at the school gates. I have worked with a retired gentleman who did not have the confidence to join a local social club. I have worked with a head teacher who has found it almost impossible to talk to the whole school in assemblies. I work with actors who feel too shy to go to some auditions because the apparent confidence of other candidates inhibits them. I work with musicians who suffer from performance nerves due to low self-confidence. I recently worked with the managing director of a national company who was losing confidence when public speaking. All found confidence.... and so can you!!

They all did the most important thing that made change possible. They took the decision to take action! They made the commitment to push on and despite apprehension, were committed to developing themselves in the knowledge that once they had achieved the confidence they desired, life would be so much better in the long-term. As human beings, we all have our limitations. The trick is to accept what we cannot change and celebrate or develop those parts of us that we can.

Defining the Barriers to Self-Confidence (and removing them)

1. Understanding Limiting Beliefs

As human beings we *think* (sometimes too much). When we are feeling positive we can often appreciate our strengths and qualities. However, if we are feeling low, we will always think negatively. We ponder on all the things we cannot achieve. We find 'reasons' why we cannot achieve what we want to, then we can blame these 'reasons' for the way we are feeling.

I'm not good at writing.

I'm too over-weight to have a boyfriend.

I'm too shy to go to parties and make new friends.

But these *reasons* for our low self-confidence are not real *reasons*, in fact we have allowed them to become *barriers* or as they are commonly known – *Limiting Beliefs.* Limiting beliefs arise due to challenging events in our lives when we have been disappointed by our performance in some way or in the behaviour of others. This event may has happened many years ago when we were children. This could be as simple as coming last in the 'egg and spoon race' at primary school! Instead of understanding that the negative experience might just have been an isolated incident, we tend to generalise that we are simply no good at some things. This may have been true at some point in the past but it does not mean it *always* has to be true. When we have negative limiting beliefs about ourselves or our abilities, we often turn them into self-fulfilling prophecies. We look for evidence that what we believe is still true and tend to ignore evidence to the contrary. However, if we begin to challenge whether these beliefs still apply and look for evidence that they may now be outdated, we begin to open up possibilities for ourselves.

Let's take Joanne's limiting belief first: *I'm too overweight to have a boyfriend.* Joanne believes that if she was a smaller size, she would instantly have all she wanted in life. Being slimmer might make Joanne feel better in the short-term, but Joanne would still feel she lacked self-confidence at times because *how* she values herself will always be the problem. Without rectifying this, no matter how slim she becomes her low self-confidence will always return.

In contrast, one of the most beautiful women I have ever met is Kayleigh. Kayleigh is 25 and is stunningly beautiful, with her long dark hair, sparkling eyes and radiant smile. She enjoys clothes and wears bright colours. She knows she is attractive and she is very comfortable in her own skin. Yet Kayleigh is a size 28 (UK dress size). This is normally considered the size of a 'larger lady' in todays' society where the average dress size in the UK is 16. She cannot always buy the clothes she wants in high street shops, and sometimes she makes them herself. Her boyfriend Dan is besotted with Kayleigh and they have been together for three years. Kayleigh and Dan are a fun-loving couple, they have a wide circle of friends and family and they are popular amongst their peers. Why wouldn't they feel confident? They are happy with what they have, and the way things are.

When I talk to Kayleigh, it is never about her weight, her size is irrelevant to how she values herself. Being a size 28 for her is *not* a 'limiting' factor. If she lost a lot of weight and became a size 12, I don't believe Kayleigh would feel any different than she does now. As a person, she is complete and totally at ease in her own skin.

So we can choose to remove our perceived barriers by changing them (i.e. losing weight) or accept and value how we look and enjoy making the best of ourselves. A confident, happy person is an attractive person! So to begin to build your confidence and to remain confident for the rest of your life you need to determine what your limiting beliefs are so that you can begin to remove them.

Limiting beliefs are often the result of long-held memories from childhood. They can be about ourselves, other people or the world in general. They are deeply rooted in our subconscious minds and guide us through our lives. By adulthood we have often stopped questioning their relevance to our current lives and have accepted them as facts. Let me share a personal example with you:

Having lost my mother at the age of six my father proceeded to move us away from the area I had known all my life and we continued to move a number of times before I became 16. This meant a number of school changes which dramatically affected my education, and eventually my exam results. I simply could not catch up, having had to re-start with a new curriculum at each school. When I left school at 16, I had some average exam results and my friends appeared to have achieved higher grades than myself. I felt 'stupid' and nothing my disappointed father had to say made me feel any different about it. Thus, believing I was 'stupid', I did not apply for college or university and began work at 16, grateful for a range of low paid jobs. Only at the age of 28 did I return to education and enter university having realised that the limiting belief that had kept me realising my potential during my early adult life was no longer relevant. What changed? Simply someone saw my potential and didn't give up on me until I took those first steps back to education. Each achievement built that self-confidence within me. I sometimes wonder, if I had not changed course, would I still be living that same life?

Exercise

Consider for a few moments those *limiting beliefs* which **you** have held about yourself, others and the world in general. Here are a few common ones:

I'm not attractive.

I'm not intelligent.

Nice men never get the girl.

Only horrible people succeed in business.

I am unlucky.

_____

_____

_____

_____

_____

_____

_____
_____
_____
_____
_____
_____
_____
_____
_____
_____

Exercise

Consider how your limiting beliefs have affected your progress over the years in your education or work, socially or
even financially. Did they prevent you from making friends,
asking someone on a date or applying for promotion?

_____
_____
_____
_____
_____
_____
_____
_____
_____
_____
_____
_____
_____
_____
_____

2. Managing Your Internal Commentary

So why is it that we allow these limiting beliefs *from way back then* to continue to determine the course of our lives? It is the fault of our *internal commentary,* which keeps these outdated beliefs alive. You know the type of thing:

I just can't do that!

What if I try to do that but fail?

How did I get that so wrong?

These destructive thinking patterns simply lead to feelings of self-doubt and failure. Taking a constructive approach to this we might equally allow ourselves some credit for what we can do, or have done well, and allow ourselves to learn from our mistakes.

I did quite well today, but how could I do that better next time?

What can I do well?

I am pleased with my progress.

As a qualified Psychotherapist and Hypnotherapist, I am aware that a positive internal commentary can help to lift your mood and propel you forward. It's a little bit like having a great supporter and friend saying, "You can do it – you know you can!" in your head.

Case Study:

I once worked with Kerry, a great hurdler who needed some help with her performance. She was on one occasion put into the senior division (aged 18 and above) of a race at the age of 15 and was extremely worried about it. She had been placed in the category because of her promising progress and it had been done to give her a further challenge and some experience running against seasoned athletes.

"I can't do it," she told me. "I will come last and be far behind the other runners, it will just be embarrassing!".

Kerry had built up her confidence in a category she knew well, with athletes of her own age, but now this situation was unknown territory for her. No matter what was discussed, it was difficult to banish this negative belief and when the gun went off and Kerry began to run, she lacked that certain 'magic' that normally characterised her performances. Kerry came fourth out of six runners and she had been very close to coming third (needless to say, I was impressed). Despite not coming last, she was disappointed by the result. It had not felt enjoyable. Of course, having felt negative about the run, she had not warmed up sufficiently and her drive to win had just not been there. I genuinely believe that if she had had belief in herself and accepted that her best efforts would be good enough, she would have taken third or second place.

On reflection Kerry realised that the race had been lost due to a limiting belief, *I can't do it!*

Had she believed; *Maybe I can do it – I'll give it a try,*

perhaps she would have prepared better and been more focussed. Eventually she did not feel disappointed due to the result – but because she knew she had placed these limitations upon herself.

Thinking negatively blocks our ability to achieve. Every negative thought we have results in a negative feeling. If we can get better at looking at the positives of being ourselves then we lift our mood and approach everything more positively. This approach can be difficult to establish if you are not used to it and requires practise. I often tell my clients to write a type of Curriculum Vitae which lists all their achievements both professional and personal no matter how small. When your read the Curriculum Vitae back occasionally, it reminds you of all your achievements and it helps to boost your confidence.

Exercise

Consider some of the negative statements you have made to yourself over the years, how could you make them more positive and supportive?

_____

_____

_____

_____

_____

_____

_____

_____

_____

_____

_____

_____

3. Stop Catastrophising

Catastrophisation is a negative thinking pattern which can habitually feed your internal commentary. It doesn't just limit you, but it can create anxiety and panic which can feel paralysing.

Catastrophic thoughts often begin with the words, 'What if'. We all have had these thoughts at one time or another.

What if I get nervous and get my words jumbled up in the interview?

What if I then begin to shake and go red?

What if my boss finds out I've been for an interview and then fires me?

What if I can't pay the mortgage and I lose my home?

These thoughts can be distressing when we catastrophise and allow thoughts like this to get out of control. When you allow catastrophic thoughts to dominate your internal commentary they have the power to bring you down. Such thoughts make us more likely to fail. They undermine us and allow us only to focus on the negatives and create fear and anxiety. If we allow these thoughts to develop unchecked they have the power to affect our performance and our ability to 'try'.

However, we can use our imaginations in a more positive way. What if we mentally rehearsed being relaxed in an interview for example?

I can see myself smiling and shaking hands with the panel.

Because I am more relaxed, I look more confident and outgoing.

I can imagine the interviewer listening intently and looking interested.

Feeling more relaxed means I can think more clearly and answer questions more proficiently.

What if I get the job – how would that feel?

What if that meant I could buy a new car?

By allowing yourself to rehearse positive images in your mind repeatedly, you allow yourself to become more relaxed and open to the possibility of a successful outcome.

4. Learning How to Accept Failure

There's a great saying – "There are no failures, only feed-back." Thomas Edison, the inventor of the domestic lightbulb took more than 10,000 attempts before he successfully produced a working lightbulb. When asked about his many failures, he said: "I have not failed. I've just found 10,000 ways that won't work."[6] Great feedback and great positivity! Experiencing failure is an essential step towards becoming self-confident.

Any successful person will tell you that they have made many mistakes over the years and these mistakes are rarely regretted. It is simply the most effective way to learn. Confident people learn to deal with those times when things go wrong and it is more about how you respond to failure than the failure itself that defines you. Failure in many ways is the only way to learn and every successful person will tell you this. Virgin boss Richard Branson is a good example of someone who is an extremely successful and wealthy entrepreneur. Yet Richard has been bankrupt at one point in his life. His response was to accept the disappointment and he began planning his next project. And who would invest in someone who had become bankrupt in business I hear you ask? Branson's confidence has seen him through the hard times and persuaded others that he has what it takes to succeed!

The value of failure as a learning opportunity cannot be overstated. I have written more about this later in this book so that you can learn from the failure and success stories of others.

5. Avoiding Making Comparisons with Others

Comparing yourself to another individual is rarely productive. When you consider that there will always be someone in the world that could arguably be more intelligent than you, or more attractive etc., it does not make sense to compare yourself to others as you are likely to damage your self-confidence and perhaps never find contentment.

However, if used positively, comparison can be a healthy and productive pastime e.g. *I ran almost as fast as them and they are more experienced than I am, I think I have done well!*

However, more often we are likely to take comparison into negative territory. *Why is she slimmer than me and yet I am sure I eat less than her! I wish I was as clever as him.*

Negative comparisons defeat us, destroy our motivation and self-esteem. Additionally, the problem with comparing yourself to others is the total waste of time and energy used in the process. Although we are bound to notice when those around us excel we rarely use this information in a positive way and perhaps as human beings, are prone to jealousy. However, if we could use comparison productively we might think more like this: *She is so good at giving presentations – perhaps I could learn from her.*

6. Tackling Fear

As a therapist and coach I work with clients struggling with anxiety every day. It is so commonplace these days that I sometimes wonder why everyone feels so alone with this issue. Anxiety and fear prevent us from doing so many things.

I'm frightened if I speak in the meeting, my hands will shake and my voice will become wobbly. Everyone will notice and it will be embarrassing.

I could not ask her out for a meal, if she says no, I might get embarrassed and look really silly.

Every time I sit in an interview, I feel so anxious, I can't think straight and cannot give professional answers to the questions.

We have probably all been there. We are in a situation where we feel completely out of our comfort zone. As we become more anxious, we question whether the decision to be at the interview was a foolish one.

I am out of my depth and they will see straight through me and realise I am not who I have suggested I am.

Anxiety is one of the most common reasons we avoid tackling new things and if we can understand anxiety and how to manage it, we can begin to build our resilience and self-confidence.

As human beings, anxiety is a perfectly normal feature of our biological make-up. In prehistoric times, when we saw a threat we would experience anxious thoughts and we would breath faster, our breaths becoming shorter. This would automatically increase the heart rate, and then our adrenaline would kick in. This was essential if we were to successfully fight the threat or run away. So anxiety and its symptoms have always served a purpose.

Today, such threats happen rarely but the demands of modern life and workplace pressures have brought about an increase in anxiety as humans struggle to cope with busy schedules and to fight increased stress. We are coping poorly as a nation simply because we are not taught how to manage this increase in pressure. However, anxiety can be managed and controlled effectively and chapter eight gives you a range of techniques and resources to help manage anxiety symptoms.

Even the most accomplished public speaker often feels a few butterflies in their stomach when they get up to speak. Susan, a speaker for a global company based in the US once told me, "I always feel a little anxious just before I get up to speak at conferences and I feel it is important to feel this way. Any performer will tell you that this improves your performance if you can simply accept it and get on with the task".

The trick to overcoming fear and anxiety is to understand that we <u>all</u> feel fearful or anxious at times. This might manifest as butterflies in the stomach, a sick feeling, a racing heart or shaking hands. The majority of people would not notice these symptoms if they were observing you but they can feel overwhelming on the inside.

7. Raising Self-Esteem

Being able to like and respect yourself is essential if you want to be liked and respected by others. Negative self-talk often focusses on the things we do not do well and it is rare that our inner voice voluntarily praises us. When you look in a mirror – what does your inner voice say? *Oh I really must get my hair cut. Is that another grey hair?*

Negative thoughts become negative feelings and bit by bit they erode our confidence. If you don't like your hair – change it! Be able to look in the mirror and say: *Oh that looks better!*

When it comes to social interaction, perfection is <u>never</u> required. You do not need to be the cleverest, most talented, most interesting or most attractive person in the room… ever! So we *can* like ourselves and celebrate our talents celebrating and accepting our imperfections.

Exercise

Think about the top three people you like best in your world. Write down the reasons why you like them. Perhaps because they are so funny, or honest or supportive:

_____
_____
_____
_____
_____
_____
_____
_____
_____
_____
_____
_____
_____
_____
_____
_____

Now ask yourself what imperfections do they have? List these also. Do those imperfections prevent you from appreciating and liking them?

_____
_____
_____
_____
_____
_____
_____
_____

_____
_____
_____
_____
_____
_____
_____

Learning to like and value yourself is important if you are to build self-confidence and remain confident in the future. It is a strange fact that we are generally quite unkind to ourselves and our own inner voice is often critical and uncaring. Acknowledging this is an important part of bringing about the change we need to enjoy being ourselves. Any Cognitive Behavioural Therapist will tell you that we all have 'automatic thoughts' and these are often negative: *What if I fail my exams? What if I can't think of anything to say at the party tonight?*

Those negative automatic thoughts, if unchallenged, result in negative feelings and these in turn bring our moods down and damage our self-confidence. Beating yourself up about your little flaws *never* results in feeling better about yourself – so it's time to try something else!

We have the choice to focus on the negatives OR the positives and by choosing to focus on the things that we like about ourselves we address the balance and think less negatively about ourselves. Be your own best friend and begin to focus on *your* talents and skills and not just on those of the people around you.

Exercise

Develop a list of things you like about yourself (this might not come easy). We have no difficulty criticizing ourselves at times, but pausing to think of the positives rarely happens. Begin to develop a list that you can add to over time. Give some examples and things you might include are: *I'm doing the best I can with the resources I have.* (You may benefit from a close friend helping you with this exercise). Keep this list and read it whenever you are having one of those negative days, to remind yourself of all the wonderful things you have to offer or that you have achieved.

_____

_____

_____

_____

_____

_____

_____

_____

_____

_____

_____

_____

_____

_____

Learning to appreciate who you are and how to be kinder to yourself will make you a happier, more content person. Standing up for your own needs and desires will also help you to be more assertive. Learning some assertiveness techniques will also help you to communicate those needs to others. How many times in the past have we felt resentful when our needs have been overlooked by another? However, if we value ourselves, we can communicate our needs and desires with others easily. When we truly value ourselves we no longer expect to settle for second best in any given situation. We would not remain in a bad relationship or horrible job simply because we would know that we deserved better. (See chapter six on assertiveness for a 'how to guide').

Self-development, In its many forms is the key to gaining self-esteem. Those people who invest in themselves add value and become more aware of their strengths. Whether this means going on a course to develop your public speaking skills or hitting the gym so that you can feel healthier. Any investment in improving yourself is very powerful and helps you to realise your potential. Learning how to maintain your car, chair a meeting, style your hair or to play tennis all would result in feeling better about yourself. Even reading a self-improvement book counts – so congratulations on taking the first step!

Personal development is about learning how things can be improved and then more importantly, taking the action to make changes. Self-development should not feel like a chore – it is about being interested in improving ourselves and enjoying the results. When we feel we have achieved something new, it can feel empowering.

Case Study:

I remember my client Bob, telling me about attending a course on *Assertiveness Skills.* At that time in his life he rarely spoke up for what he believed or wanted and often said 'Yes' to requests for his time and energy when he really wanted to say 'No!' However, he related that a one-day assertiveness course dramatically change his life for the better. The talented coach helped him to understand his own behaviours and how these behaviours were symptomatic of his feelings of low self-worth. Bob did not value his own time, so he allowed others to waste it. He did not value his own contributions in conversations, so he allowed others to talk over him. He didn't value his own needs and therefore did not speak up for himself. He began to realise how he had become often overlooked for promotion or his ideas ignored in team meetings. He had not had the self-worth at that time to say, "Hey my voice is important too!"

Having learned some assertiveness skills, when he returned to the office, he chose to give feedback about the course in the next team meeting. Perhaps he spoke a little more confidentially, because he told me that the staff listened. Or perhaps this was simply the first time that he appeared to have the conviction in himself that what he had to say was of value? He warmly warned his colleagues that he would be employing his new skills in the coming months – and he did. He began to consider what would happen if he said 'No' politely a little more often. Well of course it resulted in someone else being bogged down with more work. He noticed that he had begun to speak more in team meetings and people listened to what he had to say and valued his contributions. He realised that he must respect himself or others would not show him that respect either.

Consider the areas that you would like to improve in yourself, and why. How would improving one aspect of yourself add value or help you to enjoy life more? It might be your health, work skills, learning new hobbies or feeling better about your appearance. When you focus on how you are improving, it helps you to grow your self-confidence whereas focussing on your shortcomings can only serve to destroy your self-esteem. Those that learn the benefits of continual self-improvement learn to love the process. It is like having an injection of positivity and self-confidence every time. Embarking on a programme of self-development becomes an enjoyable pastime, we begin to enjoy the process and feel great about ourselves afterwards.

8. Zapping the Confidence Crushers

Have you noticed that being around certain people crushes your confidence? It might be a family member who criti-cizes your appearance or a colleague who always raises an error in your work during team meetings (rather that mention-ing it quietly to you beforehand). You may be aware that you are beginning to dread seeing that family member or attending the weekly team meeting because of this. Confidence crush-ers are sometimes bullies. They recognise the fact that you lack self confidence and intentionally exploit this to make themselves feel better. The interesting thing about such people is that they often lack confidence themselves and if challenged or ignored, can lose their power. However, not everyone who crushes your confidence does it intentionally and we need to consider what part we ourselves play in feeling inhibited by others.

Case Study:

May told me that whenever she visited her mother-in-law, she often made comments about her weight. Until this began,

May was fairly happy with her weight. She told me, "I wasn't the thinnest person I knew but I still felt happy with my reflection in the mirror". The comments she received ranged from, "Oh have you put on more weight recently?" to, "I've given you a smaller slice of cake darling".

May's mother-in-law Rita, was very slim and this was obviously very important to her in her own life. I don't think it had occurred to her that her son loved May as she was and did not want her to change! May began dreading visits and especially at meal times when she felt her mother-in-law was trying to restrict the portions on her plate. May's confidence had begun to plummet. She began thinking perhaps Rita was right, and perhaps she *did* need to lose weight.

When I met May she was feeling very low. As we talked through the issues, it became clear that weight gain was merely a preoccupation of Rita's solely and until Rita had mentioned it, no one had considered May's weight.

May and I worked together on managing the situation. May discussed the issue with her husband Tom and he reassured her that he thought she was perfect just the way she was. May's GP confirmed that she was a healthy weight for her height and that there were no health issues to be concerned about. Following our work, and some rehearsal, May and Tom visited Rita one afternoon inviting themselves for a chat and a coffee. After showing an interest in Rita's weekly routine, May raised the issue.

"Rita, I hope you know I respect you, and what you think about me is very important. However, I have noticed that you have made some comments about my weight recently and I want you to know that they have upset me".

Rita seemed surprised and responded, "May, I just thought I could help you to lose some weight and thought that might make you happier".

May thanked Rita politely for her concern but added, "Rita, I am very happy as I am, and my GP and Tom have assured me my weight is just fine. I really want to be relaxed and comfortable when I visit and especially when eating in front of you, so I would be really grateful if you would cease mentioning my weight or managing my portion sizes on my behalf. I know Tom will let me know if I become an unhealthy weight".

Rita was apologetic and whether it was sincere or not, did not mention weight again. May began to understand that to Rita, being slim was important to her own self-confidence, and she had been projecting this onto May. Unfortunately, she hadn't considered that this was *her own* criteria for success and she should not be trying to impose it on others. Rita learnt that her comments (although she felt they were well meaning) hurt May's feelings which was not ultimately what she had wanted to achieve. I am happy to say that Rita and May's relationship is now much better.

However, criticism sometimes can be really helpful to us providing it is constructive. The key is to no longer allow yourself to *fear* criticism. Ask yourself if the criticism is more about the other person's stress or their personal take on the world, and whether it is well meant and constructive? Without regular feedback from others we could not continually improve as people. Without May's feedback to Rita, the relationship could have become progressively worse.

But if someone continually criticizes you or makes you feel foolish intentionally, you should either avoid them or (if this is not possible) tackle their outspoken criticism next time like May did. Or perhaps you could ask for some help or support from a friend. Confidence crushers will always exist and they can steal our positive energy... don't let them!

Confidence crushers do not always *intentionally* crush your confidence. You may simply feel inhibited by a friend who you feel dresses glamorously, or who always makes everyone around you laugh. We cannot blame others for having their own self-confidence! Indeed, we should learn from these people. You might lack self-confidence around your boss because they are senior to you or because you feel they have achieved a great deal. Feeling inhibited by others often occurs due to our own low self-esteem. Tackling your low self-esteem and working on your own self-confidence will begin to help you to accept your value and no longer leave you feeling inferior in the presence of others. Remember that as human beings we are ALL equal. Do not let anyone else tell you that we are not. You should be able to sit in a room filled with millionaires, record breakers or Olympic gold medallists and by all means, be impressed and interested in their achievements, but you should never feel bad about who you are or the choices you have made!

I once watched a TV quiz show when one of the contestants was asked the usual question, "What do you do for a living?"

This lovely lady said, "I work in a fish and chip shop".

She was asked, "do you like your job?"

The lady replied in an infectiously enthusiastic manner, "Yes, I've done it all my working life, it's the best job in the world, I enjoy every single day and I meet lots of lovely people".

It struck me what a lucky lady she was, to love what she does every day… and being in the presence of a premier league footballer or millionaire could not have made her feel any differently about herself.

9. Finding the Motivation to Take Action

Who was it that said, 'Procrastination is the mother of failure'? This couldn't be truer or more important when it comes to tackling low self-confidence. As I write these words I am acutely aware that some of my readers will read this chapter and then perhaps do nothing about taking the necessary action to bring about change don't let it be you! We all struggle to get motivated at times especially if the task ahead seems difficult. There are steps you can take to improve your motivation and to achieve confidence. Use the techniques in chapter three to get you started and maintain momentum towards achieving total confidence!!

Notes

Notes

Notes

Notes

Chapter Five

First Impressions and Personal Branding – Setting the Scene for a Confident You.

Being able to behave confidently can positively determine the dynamics of any relationship, and first impressions are important as they tend to stick. You may not realise that some of the people you believe to be confident simply are *not* – they may be acting. I work with teachers, police officers and even TV personalities in order to help them to identify their unique skills and talents and to work with them to promote a confident persona when in public. The general public want their teachers to be interesting, their police to appear trustworthy and their TV personalities to be likeable. Yet despite having these qualities, my clients do not always display a consistent persona that inspires others and they need some assistance in building their personal brand which consistently shows them off in their best light. Personal branding is not about deceiving others but about giving a good 'first impression' every time and maintaining that impression moving forward. Consider what you perceive to be 'the real you' – the version of you that friends and family have grown to know and love. Even though *you* may know who you are, you may not actually reveal these aspects of your personality in the way you present yourself to others.

I once encountered a very talented photographer that struggled to get work because of the way she presented herself. I met her when I was searching for a wedding photographer for myself. We met at her studio which was in her home. When I arrived, I was shown into an untidy lounge and I remember that she wore a very untidy and ill-fitting blouse. The examples of previous wedding photos shown to me were poorly processed and loose, rather than being presented professionally in an album. I remember feeling very disappointed and did not feel I could entrust the photography of my special day to be undertaken by someone who did not understand the importance of presentation. I later discovered that the photographer had done some wonderful photography for a lucky local couple but despite this, she must have lost a great deal of potential business over the years.

It is important to consider the first impression you give to others. How would a complete stranger perceive you and your personality during a brief meeting? Think about what your true persona should look like, walk like and how would they greet people? If you want people to like you, you must think about what your appearance and behaviour says about you.

The process of *Branding* has been around for many years. Most of us understand how it helps us to identify and choose the products we trust and buy. We might buy a particular skin cream because we know it is effective on our skin and we are likely to continue to purchase it, looking out for its distinctive packaging whenever we shop. We might choose it initially because the packaging appeals to us and because its branding message appears to be reassuring us that we are buying the right product for our needs. Only when we buy it do we discover if the product works, and if it does, we may well continue to buy it for many years regardless perhaps of a higher than average price tag. As consumers we often purchase what we see as a known and trusted product every time we shop even though there may be cheaper alternatives, yet we have come to know the branded version and know what we will be getting when we open the jar.

The concept of *Personal Branding* is fairly new, but is equally important in managing first impressions and raising self-confidence. We have long understood the importance of 'first impressions' but personal branding takes this one step further. Personal branding is a process by which an individual differentiates themselves in order to stand out and succeed in business, their careers or even in their personal lives and this can be an effective way of building your self-confidence. Branding is about identifying your key competencies and unique skills and promoting these strengths to others around you in a consistent way through a number of means in order to achieve your goals. Engaging in the process of personal branding is important in finding and maintaining your self-confidence as it requires you to focus and to determine what unique skills and talents you have to offer. Then the process enables you to drive self-improvement and self-promotion in a way that is subtle and effective.

Many politicians and public figures employ professionals to help them to 'manage' their public persona essentially to be liked, trusted or respected by others and it has become an important feature in the development of their careers. However, the same principles apply whether you are aiming to develop your career, become a leader in your field or simply want to boost your self-confidence socially.

Now, consider your current 'branding' i.e. how you *appear* to the rest of the world and to decide whether the way you walk, dress, and present yourself truly portrays who you are as a person or who you want to be? This is how we not only reveal our strengths to others but also this has a huge impact on how we feel about ourselves.

Exercise

Spend a little time 'people watching'. Sit in a cafe window and watch the world go by – let your imagination go wild! Look at each person and make a mental note about your first impressions of them and who you think they might be:

Give them a name that you think suits them.

Consider where they might work or live.

How intelligent do you think they may be?

How do they dress or walk?

What do you think their hobbies or achievements might be?

Do you think they are fit and healthy?

Do you think they might be popular?

And finally… Consider this information and ask yourself this question: Would you be happy for this person to work for you or to look after your children? What does their *Personal Branding* make you feel about them?

This is a useful exercise in helping you to consider the fleeting impressions made about ourselves by others too. How can you use this experience to consider the impressions you give to others about yourself? Feedback from friends and family could be very helpful to you whilst you consider your current 'brand' and what it says about you.

Outward Appearances

Let's imagine you are working in an office in an administration role. You would like to be promoted to a management role but have not felt confident enough to have this conversation with your manager. Some days you dress smartly and other days you wear jeans to work. Your line manager however, always wears tailored suits or smart outfits and you can tell by the confident way she walks and the way she dresses and presents herself that she is a manager. She is always professional in her demeanour and in the way she speaks to others. Ask yourself - Do I look and act like a manager? The first step towards promotion is looking the part, whether it is the attention you pay to your appearance or the way you walk or talk to colleagues. Think about your own circumstances - do you present yourself in a way which makes you feel self-confident? Does the way you dress make the most of your good points? Remember that when a tourist board promotes a holiday destination in a TV advert they always show the world its beaches on hot sunny days and not in the rain or when they are over-crowded. The advert promotes all the great things the country has to offer and does not reveal the worst aspects. Stand up tall, shoulders back, smile and make eye contact - all these things are the mark of a confident person. Take time to talk audibly and ensure you do not talk too quickly which may reveal some anxiety and may result in you feeling breathless. When you APPEAR confident more people will treat you with respect, and this often results in you FEELING confident.

Give some thought to your personal branding. If you arrive for an interview wanting to impress and looking amazing in a smart suit, immaculate shoes, hair and nails etc. but you are driving your faithful but tired old car – simply park it around the corner. However, equally think about how you talk and communicate with others, well written correspondence says a great deal about you. Having defined your goals you can determine how the new successful *you* should look. Work towards achieving that unique look and behaviour, which will help others understand the real you and to see your best points.

It is worth focussing on the power of first impressions for a moment. It is believed that a first impression is made within the first three seconds of meeting someone and that from this point onwards it becomes difficult to change a person's perception. Think carefully about the first impressions you make on others. The way we dress, behave and communicate has a powerful effect on how we are perceived, and we can make this work for us! Of course, once the first three seconds have passed we do have the opportunity for people to get to know us better. However, a bad first impression can be difficult to rectify.

Acting Confident

At this point you may be reading this and thinking *I don't want to _act_ confident – I want to _be_ confident!* However, acting as if you are confident is in fact one powerful way of *actually beginning to _feel_* confident. This is how it works:

I was once invited to a group interview for a media job many years ago, I had done everything I could to look the part, but like anyone else would be, felt a little nervous beforehand. I dressed like the staff featured in their website and had done a great deal of research. The staff dressed in the company's colours of black, white and red and I had taken the decision to wear a black suit, white shirt and red tie on the day in the hope that it would make me 'look the part'. When I entered the room there were a number of candidates already seated and as I entered, I walked confidently, smiled at everyone and greeted them with a warm 'good morning'. As I sat down, I became aware that the other candidates had all turned 'expectantly' towards me and clearly were confused as to who I was and whether I was part of the interview panel, and one candidate asked me the same. I smiled at them all and reassured them, "No, no… I am just another candidate like you".

That first impression had had a surprising effect. When I spoke during the group tasks, I found other candidates in the room listened to me and often deferred to me. My apparent self-confidence had clearly had an impact on the confidence of others around me. Their behaviour towards me boosted my self-confidence further and I did go on to secure the job offer. I was later told by my new employer, "You were an outstanding candidate. From the minute we met, you looked like you were part of the team already and you talked confidently throughout the interview".

When I started on my first day, I felt I had achieved a certain amount of respect already which made meeting others and settling into the role easier. I am aware that there were other candidates in the room that day that had higher qualifications, and some had a good deal more experience. However, my apparent self-confidence had clearly led to some of the candidates giving up before they had even begun. The simple fact is that if you *act* confident people treat you differently and that helps you to *feel* more confident.

So when we are goal setting we need to determine who we are, deep down, and what we wish to share with the world. Understand that people have very little to go on when deciding what they think of you in those first three seconds. How you dress, communicate, walk etc. can have an impact on how you feel about yourself and how others perceive you. Make sure that first impression allows others see the 'real you'. If you do decide to try a new look, although it may be daunting at first, you will get used to seeing yourself in a different way very quickly.

Now I understand that some of you may be thinking that 'acting confident' would be difficult for you to achieve. The important thing is to practise the technique. Experiment with the way you dress/walk/communicate when you call into a local shop or when you ask directions. These are all people you will probably never meet again, and what they think is not of prime importance to you. However, getting used to engaging with others, smiling, chatting and beginning to build your self-confidence slowly in these areas can be achieved in this way.

Are you struggling to feel you can look how you want to look? Invest some time and thought into the improvements you can make to yourself that you know would make a difference to how you feel. This is not about being the most attractive person in the room but it is about you feeling good in your own skin so losing a few pounds or changing your hairstyle or hair colour could make a huge difference. It is vital to get advice and feedback from others – ask your hairstylist or friend for advice. Have a look on the internet for people whose style you admire, cut out photos and get some feedback before and after from others. This will help you to make bolder decisions and feel happier with the changes you make. I once asked a lady in the street if I could photograph her hairstyle so that I could later show it to my hairdresser. Of course, she was delighted to help and said I had boosted her self-confidence!

Case Study of a Personal Branding Exercise:

Sonya wanted to be a Visual Marketing Consultant for a London fashion outlet. She had trained in design and had all the necessary qualifications but lacked the experience. On the first occasion that I met her I noticed that she walked up to my office door with her shoulders and head down moving in an unsure and timid manner. She looked quite young and vulnerable.

We began to consider what a professional visual marketing consultant might look like! We looked at the portfolios of successful consultants online and Sonya decided which examples of branding might represent who she truly was and we began to make some changes and to improve her self-confidence. Professional fashion consultants have portfolio's! Sonya did not have one as she had never previously valued her work.

We worked together on approaching a few local companies in order to offer them some 'free visual marketing services' and Sonya spent a few weeks improving the layout and visual aspects of these stores in return for a testimonial about her work and the opportunity to photograph the results. She used some fresh and radical approaches and she was able to put together a wonderful portfolio of her work to impress prospective employers.

By her own admission, Sonya did not 'look like' a visual marketing consultant for the fashion industry. She began to buy some key items for her wardrobe which made her 'feel the part' and changed her hairstyle from long hair tied back in a ponytail, to a short bob which made her look more 'business-like'. Sonya arrived for one of our sessions wearing her 'new look' and the transformation was phenomenal. Of course, the new clothes and hairstyle made a marked and positive difference, but more surprising was the way she walked and presented herself. She walked tall, shoulders back striding purposely, and when our eyes met, she smiled a super beaming smile. She looked more mature, and a great deal more confident. She told me that just wearing the clothes she loved helped her to feel she was dressing as her *true self,* presenting herself outwardly in a way which demonstrated her personality. She came the following week with professionally applied makeup having had a makeup lesson at the local salon. Sonya's confidence just grew and grew as people began to see the 'real her' which had been hidden inside for so long. I'm not sure if Sonya got that job in visual marketing but I don't think that really matters! Having a goal helped Sonya to take the important steps towards finding her true self and letting the world see who she really was.

Exercise

Take some time out and return to the activity of people-watching. I would like you to imagine you plan to recruit a gardener, hairstylist or advertising manager. From the first impressions you form of people who walk by and their personal branding, who would look the part?

Why do they inspire you?

Do they look like a professional?

Do they look confident and self-assured?

Think about the next career role you would like to achieve, people-watch until you find someone who looks like the perfect candidate. What impresses you about them?

How do they dress, walk, carry themselves?

How could this information help you to develop your own personal brand?

Notes

Notes

Notes

Chapter Six

Assertiveness

Confident people are usually *assertive* and this is an attribute, and skill that if mastered, and added to your programme of self-development, will build and maintain your confidence moving forward.

If you are assertive, you have the ability to state your opinion or express your needs and rights in an outwardly confident manner. Assertive people behave in a way that expresses their confidence and this can command respect.

Assertiveness is sometimes confused with *Aggressive* or *Bullish* behaviour but real assertiveness could not be more different. If you are assertive, you stand up for your right to be treated respectfully and fairly by others in a positive and polite way. An assertive person can express their own opinions, needs and feelings without ignoring those of others. However, because most people want to be liked and respected, (especially those who lack self-confidence), we often put the needs and desires of others first and avoid expressing our own needs or opinions especially if they conflict with others. When we fail to have respect for our own needs, opinions or feelings, others do the same and this can lead to being mistreated or taken for granted. Of course, why would others value us if we do not value ourselves?

Assertive people are comfortable with refusing the requests of others if they are inconvenient or too demanding. They are comfortable making requests, sharing opinions, questioning rules or traditions politely, addressing problems and being firm so that their rights are respected and they are able to express how they feel to others.

Many of the clients I work with struggle to be assertive. They fear that if they stand up for themselves or say 'No' to an unreasonable request, they will offend the other person. Rather than do this, they often say nothing. But saying nothing breeds resentment and often ends relationships.

Case Study:

Fin was 33 when we met and he was having difficulty saying 'No' to the growing list of requests he was receiving from his mother, Beth. Fin's father had died some two years earlier and in a bid to support his mother who he loved, he had stepped in to help her with many of the issues that arose around her home, like changing light bulbs or employing tradesmen. These were all tasks that his father has once undertaken and when they needed doing in the early days following his father's death, Fin was happy to step in and assist. However, as time went on Beth began to perceive all these tasks as being part of Fin's role as a son. Her requests changed from, "I can't figure out how to change this light bulb… could you help me next time you visit," to, "You need to come tonight to change my light bulb!" Enquiries became expectations and Fin felt his mother had taken his kindness for granted. Fin had two young children and a wife who struggled with health issues and as a family man, working long hours, his time was limited. He began to dread the phone calls and requests and this began to place a strain on his feelings for his mother.

I began to work with Fin by discussing the level of support which he felt would be reasonable for him to provide and (as Beth was just 60 years of age and in a fairly good state of health) what duties she might begin to take on herself. Beth was retired and I believe, lonely and bored. She was still understandably grieving for the loss of her husband and so asking her son to come to the house to change a light bulb gave her some company in the evenings so the number of requests had naturally grown over time. Fin began to visit his mother's home most evenings and this was impacting negatively on his well-being as he struggled to find time for himself and his family.

At the time, I believe Beth had not considered Fin's position at all and was unlikely to unless he shared his thoughts and feelings with her. Apparently, Beth later admitted that she had realised it was probably inconvenient for him at times, but that she just felt she needed the support. As he always agreed to help out, she did not question her actions.

Fin and I began to plan an assertive conversation between himself and Beth. Fin was very anxious about potentially upsetting his mother and it was important for him to let her know that he would always be there to support her when she needed it. However, he wanted her to know that he did not have enough time available in the day to be an employee, husband, father and to perform many of his late father's duties. Fin began by calling her to say he would be around later that day and that he needed to speak to her about something very important. By doing this, Fin now felt committed to having the conversation and Beth was ready and curious to hear what he had to say.

Using our notes, Fin worked through the list of things he needed to impart that day. It was something along these lines:

"Mum, it is really important to me that you know I love you and enjoy coming to see you and that I will always support you and that will never change. However, I have realised that dropping in every day is putting a strain on the precious free time I have and means I do not always see the children before bedtime or am able to see friends in the evenings. I know it has been hard for you not to have Dad around, but I now feel we have to find a 'new normality' where we can all manage this loss. You have not met friends or done a great deal over the last two years and I believe you now need to begin to find some independence, interests and enjoyment outside of your home. I will help and support you to do that so that you need never feel alone. Also, as you have a good pension, I will support you to find trustworthy tradespeople who can cut your grass or maintain your home so that it is no longer a worry for you, but I cannot do that work as often myself as my own home needs my time also."

When Fin spoke to Beth about his feelings, she was I believe, a little emotional and very surprised by Fin's assertiveness. He had voiced a clear and concise (and gentle) statement of his intent and this enabled them to move forward planning that *new normality* together. Beth developed a new appreciation for the support Fin gave her and Fin's family life improved.

Case Study – Debbie:

Debbie worked in administration and finance for a large insurance company when she came to see me, and she was suffering from extreme workplace stress. The stress had been having an impact on her sleep and she was feeling overwhelmed.

When we chatted about the issues, it became apparent that other colleagues in the office did not appear to be as stressed as Debbie herself. She told me that the manager always gave her more work than the others and that her in-tray was always full. However, Debbie stated that she never refused to complete tasks, as she felt she did not want to appear unhelpful or to annoy the manager. Eventually, Debbie felt very angry one day when she had to leave work late in order to finish some work, being aware that a colleague (Kate), had taken two hours for lunch yet had left on time.

Debbie and I worked together on an assertive approach to resolve the situation. The following week, Debbie did an assessment of the work she had in her in-tray first thing on Monday morning. She was pretty sure it would take most of the day. When her manager came along with a new piece of work which he required to be completed for the afternoon, she dealt with this assertively yet politely.

'Ahh, I'm not sure I can take this one Mark! I have assessed all I have in my in-tray already, all the jobs are marked 'urgent' and I know this work will take most of the day. I would hate for the work not to be completed if it is for an important customer. If this is an important job, is there anyone else you could ask to do it? Or is there anything else in the tray that could wait?'

Mark looked through the other items in her tray and agreed she had a lot to do, he then placed the new piece of work in Kate's tray. He became more aware of Debbie's workload and often asked her about her availability before giving her work from then on.

You have to practice assertiveness for it to become a habit. If you are that friend that can never say 'No' to babysitting the neighbour's children then you will always be the first person they rely on to step in at short notice. You must practise saying, "I'm sorry I simply can't do it this evening" – no need to give an explanation!

If you are assertive, people naturally respect your time and your assistance and will no longer take you 'for granted'. This will dramatically strengthen your confidence. Remember your time, energy, opinions and feelings are just as important as those of everyone else!!

Try completing the questions below – If you answer YES to more than five then taking time out to practise assertiveness skills would benefit you. There are lots of books on assertiveness skills available on the market, consider buying one to help you with your self-development and never feel taken for granted again!

Exercise

How Assertive are You?

Consider the questions below and determine how many you can say 'yes' to:

1. Have you ever agreed to do something for someone and felt resentful about it afterwards?

2. If your boss asks you directly to take on a piece of work, do you <u>always</u> say 'YES'?

3. A friend asks you to go out for a drink and you say 'NO' because you feel tired – Would you feel guilty?

4. A work colleague habitually calls you in tears just as you are about to go to bed – Do you stay up for as long as they need to support them foregoing your much-needed sleep?

5. You are aware that you have been given more than your fair share of work by your manager, would you feel silently annoyed but unable to query why?

6. A family member decides that there should be a family party and states it would be best held at your home as you 'have the biggest lounge'. Do you feel 'taken for granted' yet unable to say anything for fear of upsetting someone?

7. Your disorganised neighbour asks you if you could babysit at short notice this evening for the third time in a few weeks. You had fancied a quiet night in watching your favourite film and soaking in the bath. Would you cancel your plans?

8. Your work colleague keeps taking extended lunch hours and leaving you to cover the phones. Would you avoid challenging her behaviour for fear of falling out with her?

9. Your friend asks you to spend a weekend helping her to move house and you agree although you know she would never give you that support herself?

10. A family member regularly asks you to pick up things for them whilst you are out shopping. You

don't mind helping them, but it always involves going out of your way to deliver them to her on your way home?

Without doubt, you can boost your personal confidence by being more assertive with those around you, in the home, at work, the shop counter, anywhere where you feel your needs must be clearly and respectfully shared with others. Your assertiveness can be greatly enhanced if you can adopt some of the following techniques into your communications with others.

Personal Space: Do not allow yourself to feel uncomfortable or intimated by someone invading your personal space. Take a step to the side or a step backwards in order to find that space where you feel comfortable. Invading an individual's personal space can indicate passive aggressive behaviour and is manipulative and intimidating, so move away or ask them, politely, to move away from you.

Plan ahead: If you plan to be assertive with someone, spend some minutes beforehand thinking about what it is you want to say. What is it that you want? Consider if it is fair for you to ask for what you need, what words you should use to express your needs clearly and to make yourself understood.

Eye Contact: Maintain eye contact through most of the conversation to demonstrate you are focussed on the other person. If you look down throughout a conversation you risk appearing nervous or dishonest. Try to get a good balance ensuring that you maintain eye contact when challenging someone.

Conversation Tips

Use positive *opening statements*: Begin by setting the tone for a productive conversation and perhaps getting the other person 'on board' with the right opening line. Try something complimentary such as, "I really appreciate you letting me talk to you about this," or, "I could really do with your help and advice on this".

If you begin a conversation with a question i.e., "is it okay if I ask you a question?" by them saying, "yes," they have just given you permission to ask whatever it is you want to ask. For example:

"Do you mind if I ask you something?"

"No problem. What can I do for you?"

"When would it be convenient for us to sit down and talk about that salary increase you mentioned last month?"

This is more effective than

"I need to talk to you about my wages!!!"

Apologies: If there has been an incident in the recent past for which the person you are about to speak to might deserve an apology from you, then do it at the start and get it out of the way before you start to express your need. Even though they may be saying something that is in opposition to what you need, let them know that you understand why they feel the way they do. There is more chance of them listening and understanding you if you can let them know that you, in turn, are listening and understanding them.

Body Language: Once you have planned what you want to say, keeping the individual outside of your personal space, you can keep eye contact and give them your opening statement. Using your body language communicate to the other person what you need. If you are standing, do not slouch as it will make you look smaller and less confident, if you are sitting, do not cross your arms and/or legs as it may make you look defensive or confrontational.

Speech: Resist the temptation to speak too quickly. Speaking in a low pitch at a slower pace shows that you are in control of your emotions and believe in what you are saying. A high pitch would betray you as being fearful, insecure or nervous. When necessary, take a couple of deep breaths to get you back on track. Listen to what the other person says and without interrupting them, repeat, some of the important points to demonstrate you have been listening. This will signify that you have understood their perspective and reinforces your assertiveness.

Reinforcing your message: If you encounter resistance to the message you are trying to get across because the other party will not listen, repeat the message, then if necessary, repeat it again. Eventually your message will get through. However this technique, though it is effective is best used in one-off situations because using this technique at home or at work regularly could cause irritation. If you find yourself in the mobile phone shop helping an elderly relative buy a 'simple to use' basic mobile phone, but the salesperson wants to sell you a top of the range android hyper connected blah blah blah… tell him again that you simply want a basic phone. When they then try to tell you how much music your 84-year-old relative can download onto the top of the range one… tell them again. Eventually they will get the message and your relative will get the phone they need.

Practise: It is important to understand that practising assertiveness skills can be vital if they are to work. The first time you are *assertive* can feel uncomfortable, especially with someone who you have struggled to communicate with in the past. The person who is used to hearing you say 'Yes' might be shocked when you say 'No' for the first time. Try not to show your discomfort and cheerfully change the subject as soon as possible demonstrating that your refusal is not personal and you are still amicable. It will get easier each time you try and the wonderful thing about assertiveness is that when you have been assertive once or twice with someone, they generally respect and value your time and efforts and will not have the same disregard for you in future.

Evaluate and Celebrate: It is important to understand that even the *assertive confident you* may not get *all* of your needs met *all* of the time. So after you have been assertive with someone, evaluate what you did well and consider where you might make improvements in the future. Practice those areas which require improvement and begin to develop and refine your skills. When you next find yourself in a situation where you have felt the need to be assertive and you are happy with the outcome, knowing that your own needs were met whilst respecting the needs of others, then give yourself a pat on the back. You deserve it!!

Notes

Notes

Notes

Chapter Seven

The Value of Failure

*"Failure is only the opportunity more intelligently
to begin again" Henry T Ford*[7]

One of the most important lessons you can learn from this book is how to embrace failure! As human beings all our learnings are a result of trial and error and without failure we would learn nothing from our experiences. I passed my driving test after the third attempt. Of course, at times it was disappointing and frustrating. However, what I gained from each experience were the skills I needed to improve and to be a better driver. So if you fail an exam, and your tutor gives you valuable feedback, you will be one step nearer to passing the exam next time as you will be better informed and educated about where things went wrong. This means your chances of success will be higher. Not everything we wish to achieve will happen immediately, so if you want to pass that exam, keep learning and keep going back until you *have* passed!!

*"Winners never quit and quitters never win!!"
Vince Lombardi*[8]

However, my work informs me that many of us do quit when we fail at something because we perhaps feel embarrassed or defeated. Perhaps it feels like a confirmation that we really are not up to the task. Whatever the reason for failure on a single occasion, what defines you as a person is not the odd failure along the way, but your determination to 'push on' and get there in the end. Tackling defeat in this way earns respect from those around you. Seeing failure for what it is, a temporary setback, enables you to move on to achieving success. Once you understand this principal you might be frustrated by temporary setbacks but they will no longer permanently defeat you.

> *"Never confuse a single defeat with a final defeat"*
> *F. Scott Fitzgerald*[9]

Failure is such a final word. It implies that there is 'no going back' no chance to 'make good' on those aspirations you have for yourself. But actually failure is a small step which better prepares you for the next phase. Utilising your positive inner voice, you must allow a little time for reflection following the set-back but then get back on track, using the knowledge you have gained through failure to achieve more next time. When Thomas Edison designed the light bulb, it took a great many attempts to make electric light possible. Thank goodness he persevered!

> *"I have not failed. I've just found 10,000 ways*
> *that it won't work" Thomas A. Edison*[10]

So if you fail your driving test or do not get that job offer, it is vital you ask for feedback! Feedback is the optimum opportunity to learn from your experience. Are you carrying out a driving manoeuvre incorrectly or are you saying the wrong thing in interview situations? You need this valuable information so that you can refine your performance for next time. Do not allow yourself to feel upset or angry by the feedback you receive, it is the biggest favour that a person can give you, be grateful for it! So, if an interviewer tells you that you were inappropriately dressed for an interview, refrain from taking offence. This has been their genuine first impression of you and it helps you to understand how you are perceived by others who don't know you. Take the feedback on board, ask for advice, and get the most out of this situation as it will help you to confidently attend the next interview feeling better prepared.

One of the best things about failures along the route to success is the way you feel when you finally lift that trophy, accept that job offer or pass that qualification. Having the drive to keep going when things felt difficult, and to bounce back from the setbacks will help to build your self-confidence and your resilience for the future. You will be able to look back and feel proud of your tenacity and be aware when moving forward with your life that you *can* succeed. You can feel good about yourself and your achievements and they feel all the more deserved and valuable when they didn't come easy. This can have a positive impact on how you feel about yourself and how others perceive you.

> *"Failure is the condiment that gives success its flavour" Truman Capote*[11]

There are many successful people who have comfortably talked about their failures on the way to success. J.K. Rowling, author of the amazing Harry Potter books has been interviewed many times and talked about the setbacks she has experienced along the way, but she kept going, and became one of the world's most successful authors. Seven years from her graduation day, her marriage had ended and she was an unemployed single mother. Life was a struggle for quite some time as she forged a new life for herself and her child but she is clear today about the benefits of failure.

Richard Branson is another successful man who has shared his own experiences of failure and setbacks and understands the educational value of those failures. Over the years he has launched a number of companies that have succeeded and some that have failed, and like any true entrepreneur has learned from those experiences.

"You don't learn to walk by following rules. You learn by doing, and by falling over." Richard Branson[12]

We all fail to achieve what we set out to achieve at times. The important thing is how we respond to this failure – do we see it as a barrier or a stepping stone?

Case Study:

Beau had applied for the role of Air Cabin Crew for one of the top airlines. The airline is renowned for being very particular about the people they employ and they hold open days each year to select suitable candidates. There are a number of stages you must pass through before you can even achieve an interview and Beau had failed three times to get to that interview stage. However, through the work we did together, she began to realise that she was becoming more knowledgeable about the process each time, what the expectations were and how to tackle the exercises used for selection purposes. When I first met Beau she was struggling to motivate herself to attend the fourth selection day.

She had been accepted for an interview on the last selection day some months beforehand, but did not get through the process. However, on the fourth occasion Beau did indeed get the job offer she desired. She now recognises that each stage was a learning opportunity and without those 'failures' she would not have learnt what she had needed to do, in order to get fully through the process. She no longer sees these previous disappointments as 'failures' but as 'stepping stones' to finding her dream job.

Exercise

Think of three times in your past when you failed to achieve what you had set out to achieve. Perhaps this was the first time you ran in sports day at school, or tried to ride a bicycle, or was it failing a driving test or missing out on a job opportunity?

What did you learn from each failure?

Did you use this learning productively?

Can you remember a time when you failed to achieve something and refused to try again?

What might have happened if you had persevered?

Has fear of failure prevented you from having or doing something you would like to achieve?

Case Study:

Matt had tried and failed to pass his driving test seven times when we met and he was desperate to change things. After the first two tests he had begun to focus so much on what might go wrong, that this damaged his self-confidence each and every time.

"I just can't pass a driving test" he told me.

We decided to put his driving lessons on hold for two weeks in order to focus on what I felt was the main reason he had continued to fail – his fear of failure and resulting lack of self-confidence.

When we analysed why Matt had failed each test, the reasons had been different each time. One time his parking was perfect, but then the next he might fail on this part of the test. Another time he was told he wasn't checking in his mirrors enough, the next they said he checked them too often. He had found himself in a very anxious and negative state of mind.

Feeling positive when you embark on something that tests or challenges you is very important and will help you to succeed. When you feel confident taking your driving test, your mind and body are more relaxed. This means:

You are able to remember what you have learnt more effectively.

You are able to think more clearly and make better judgements.

You are able to understand and respond to requests more quickly.

You trust yourself to get things right and this takes some pressure off you.

Your body is less tense and can operate the car more effectively.

But how does one take their eighth driving test and arrive feeling confident after so much disappointment? Becoming resilient in this situation was of paramount importance. First of all Matt needed to *accept* what had been continuing to happen. For Matt this was:

a. Matt had failed his driving test seven times.
b. He was feeling low and demoralised and had developed a limiting belief – *I will never pass my driving test!*
c. He had passed all aspects of the curriculum at some point so he *did* know how to drive.
d. Matt still wanted to pass his driving test.

Accepting these points helped Matt to refocus on the task in hand. He recognised that arriving for the test in a negative frame of mind made him feel nervous and he doubted himself throughout every task, which was distracting and demotivating. He agreed that taking his test in this frame of mind was not productive and this helped us to move forward and let go of the past. Matt later agreed to do the following:

a. To take his test as many times as it took in order to pass.
b. To continue to learn and test himself against the test curriculum to retain all that he had learned to date.
c. Instead of worrying about failure, Matt would focus on what he could do before the test to relax his nerves and his body.
d. During the test he would listen intently to the examiners instructions and not allow himself to think about anything other than what he needed to do.

e.   He would accept that he may fail next time but as long as he kept trying – he *would* pass at some point.

Focussing on these points helped Matt to feel more resilient. We no longer talked about 'if' he passed his driving test but 'when' he would pass. We talked about what car he would buy and how he might celebrate. When he took the next driving test he prepared himself well. He was focussed on doing the best he could and did not think about passing or failing. He had come to accept that he *would* pass his test at some point, it was just a matter of time!

Of course, Matt passed the very next time he took the test. Having been in the test scenario so many times, he knew exactly what to expect and was far better prepared than someone taking the test for the first time. He had felt calmer and accepting of the situation he had found himself in, which meant he had been better able to focus on what he was required to do.

Exercise

Think of something you have failed to achieve in the past. How did it make you feel and what limiting belief did it produce? i.e. did you struggle to speak in public or did you burn yet another birthday cake?

_____
_____
_____
_____
_____
_____

_____

_____

_____

_____

_____

_____

_____

_____

_____

_____

Use Matt's case study to help you logically plan how you could overcome these experiences moving forward. What did you learn from them?

Notes

Notes

Notes

Chapter Eight

Techniques and Strategies to Help You Manage Anxiety

Anyone who suffers from a lack of confidence will have experienced the crippling effects of anxiety whenever they have been forced to step out of their comfort zone. The symptoms of anxiety can range from a niggling feeling of self-doubt or fear, to more extreme levels resulting in panic attacks when one might experience heart palpitations and experience nausea. Many of the clients I work with have avoided situations for many years which bring about symptoms of anxiety and this has limited their ability to live the lives they would like to live. It has even prevented them from achieving their dreams. They would love to be a performer but are afraid of standing on stage in front of others, or they want to apply for a promotion at work but are afraid of failure.

When we step out of our comfort zone, anxiety or apprehension is perhaps to be expected, but as we have already discussed, this feeling is a normal human reaction to experiencing something new and a little more challenging.

There are a few things you can do to lessen the symptoms of anxiety which may assist you when things get a little challenging along the journey to achieving your goals. Try out a few techniques below and monitor the impact these have on your anxiety. Find something that works for you and use it regularly whether you feel anxious, or not, to maintain a permanent state of calm. Recognising that you are able to utilise a range of techniques to manage anxiety is empowering and will help you to leave the fear behind and to build self-confidence.

Cognitive Behavioural Therapy

Cognitive Behavioural Therapy (CBT) is a psychotherapeutic approach to managing unhelpful, negative and distressing thoughts often referred to as 'thinking errors.' We all have automatic thoughts which pop into our minds throughout the day and sometimes these thoughts can be negative e.g.

Oh no, I forgot to put the washing out on the line before I went to work.

Or

I have failed to get the job from the last three interviews.

Such thoughts tend to be the beginning of a negative spiral which in-turn has an impact on how we feel. Although these thoughts are quite natural, how we manage them can be very important. Many of us are unaware of the impact of these automatic thoughts on our mood, self-confidence and self-esteem.

A destructive pattern can develop from one negative thought and if the thought is not challenged, it can develop and create more negativity and low self-confidence. This is how it develops:

Oh no, I forgot to put the washing out on the line this morning.

I promised Sal I would do it last night.

That means I won't get the clothes dry until Wednesday.

I'm such an idiot. It's the third time I've forgotten this week and Sal is going to be really angry.

Or...

I have failed at the last three interviews...

I'm never going to get a job!

I must not be cut out to be a Project Manager and perhaps everyone knows that.

I'm such a failure.

Negative thinking is not helpful and can spiral out of control leaving you feeling despondent and low. Feeling that way affects your motivation and damages your self-confidence. It also means that next time you go to an interview, there is a good chance you will feel more anxious the night before or during the interview itself.

CBT techniques can help you to tackle your negative thoughts immediately each time they occur ensuring a more positive and productive outcome. Taking positive action helps you to accept the inevitability of your 'pop-up' thoughts and to build your self-confidence. Let's see how the two earlier examples could have been tackled more positively producing a better outcome and a more positive impact on mood and self-confidence:

Oh no… I've forgotten to put the washing out on the line again this morning!

I wonder why I simply cannot remember to do it?

Tonight, I will place a sticky note on my briefcase and as soon as I pick it up to go to work tomorrow I will remember I need to hang the washing out first.

I'll text Sal right now to apologise and tell her about my reminder plan.

Or

I have failed to get a job from the last three interviews.

I am however getting to the interview stage which is pretty good.

I wonder if I could get some help from a mentor to improve my interview technique or call the companies to find out why I was unsuccessful and get some feedback. Perhaps they could give me some ideas about how I might improve my technique for the future?

If I keep improving, surely I will get a new job in the end.

By challenging our negative thoughts we are able to change the pattern of thoughts and begin thinking in a much more productive way. Feeling more positive about ourselves and our abilities reduces anxiety. If we go to the next interview believing we are getting better all the time and really <u>do</u> have a chance of getting the job, our chances of doing so increase.

A cognitive approach assists you to manage your thoughts more positively and to avoid developing limiting beliefs *e.g. I will never get a new job!* People who practice CBT look at the evidence for many of the negative thoughts they have to determine whether they are true or relevant to them i.e.:

Am I capable of passing my driving test?

How many people do I know that have passed their driving test? Are they really all more 'capable' than me?

Did they all pass first time?

My driving instructor said he put me in for my test because he felt I was ready.

The chances are that if I learn from each mistake I make, I will eventually know all I need to know about how to drive and I will be able to demonstrate this to the examiner.

Challenging the thought process reveals that many of our automatic thoughts are incorrect and are created to reflect our own fears and low self-esteem. By being proactive in challenging these harmful thoughts we are able to balance our thinking and see our successes as well as our failures.

You can learn more about CBT techniques by working with a CBT therapist, attending a course or simply learn some strategies from a reputable CBT book.

Exercise

Choose the most productive and helpful CBT response to the following negative events:

The new puppy has made a mess in the kitchen again.

1. *I'm sick and tired of cleaning up after this puppy.*
2. *Where can I get puppy training lessons?*
3. *I'm sorry but we cannot keep this puppy if it's going to make all this mess.*

Your favourite jeans no longer fit.

1. *I need to buy some new jeans but I cannot afford them. I'll have to stay in tonight.*
2. *These jeans have shrunk in the wash.*
3. *This is just the incentive I needed to get back on to my diet and get fitter and healthier.*

Mindfulness

Mindfulness is a psychological process which has its roots within Buddhism. It is the process of bringing one's attention and consciousness into the here and now (the present) rather than focussing on events from the past or indeed concerning ourselves with the future. It is generally believed to have been introduced to the west by Jon Kabat-Zinn and is used to achieve inner peacefulness and self-knowledge.

If you feel stressed or anxious, your thoughts are generally focussed on events from the past (perhaps thinking about something that went wrong) or in the future (worrying about what might go wrong). However, when our thoughts are in the here and now we are generally calmer, as we are focussed on doing something proactively. Mindfulness is about keeping your thoughts in the present for a little while, putting everyday life on hold for just a few minutes. When we invest our time in this calming activity we leave behind negative thoughts which fuel anxiety and let go of anxious thoughts. This can be done by attending a Mindfulness class or listening to a Mindfulness Meditation CD or phone app. A calm and soothing voice will guide you through a breathing exercise to help you slow your breathing and this allows your heart rate to drop. When this occurs we feel calm and 'in control'. It's a super way of remaining calm and unstressed and can be done almost anywhere and almost any time.

You could listen to a Mindfulness app before going on a date or on the morning of an interview to help you think more clearly and to manage interview nerves or to relax at the end of a stressful work day. You can also use Mind-fulness in the evenings to help you to unwind and achieve improved sleep quality. You can try some Mindfulness meditations for free by visiting the Confidence Guru website www.confidenceguru.com.

Relaxation Classes

Whether it's Yoga, Tai Chi, Pilates, or even Meditation, taking a weekly class can be a good way of releasing tension and improving your wellbeing. Taking some time out simply to achieve that 'me time' will help you to become accustomed to leaving the stress of normal life behind, if only for an hour. The class gives you the opportunity to focus on your own physical or psychological wellbeing and you will feel the benefit of this almost immediately.

If you are unable to attend a class, you could consider purchasing a relaxation DVD of any of the above activities so that you can use the techniques at home when you feel stressed or anxious. Learning to 'let go' and relax is a skill we all need to learn but once mastered it can be a reliable tool to help us to manage the anxiety we feel when we step out of our comfort zone.

Exercise

Most of us are aware of the importance of exercise in promoting good mental health and wellbeing. However, if you work full time and have other responsibilities, it can be difficult to fit this in around a busy schedule. Note that, anything you can achieve here is better than nothing at all and going for a 20 minute walk each weekend or walking to work once a week would all contribute to your physical and mental wellbeing and can assist in keeping anxiety at bay.

Exercise can be easier to achieve if you can encourage others to join you, so try to think about ways in which you might do something active with your partner or family.

Hypnotherapy

Hypnotherapy is a common approach used in tackling fears and phobias, but it can also be very useful in managing anxiety. Hypnotherapy is a therapeutic technique which helps the client to harness their own willpower and inner resources and at all times the client is in full control. Indeed, therapist and client work together to bring about the client's desired outcome. It is the therapist's role to create the conditions and resources for this desired change and to ensure that you feel safe and secure and they will guide and support you throughout the whole experience.

The state of hypnosis is a natural one and the therapist takes you through a simple process to help you to achieve a natural state of physical, mental and emotional relaxation, along with a heightened state of awareness. When experiencing hypnotherapy, the unconscious mind becomes more aware of and more receptive to inner emotions and issues together with positive thoughts, ideas and concepts. This helps the client to harness their own willpower and inner resources to bring about positive change.

The change of consciousness brought about by hypnotherapy is extremely comfortable and relaxing and you will recognise the feeling as it is experienced naturally by everyone in their daily lives. Everyone has experienced this trance-like state (although they may not have realised it), when daydreaming, reading, or even driving. Have you ever driven to a familiar destination and realised you can't remember any of the journey? Or have you ever been so caught up in a TV programme or a book and discovered you have lost track of time? The experience is a calming combination of hyper-focussed thought and general relaxation.

A hypnotherapist can work with you to achieve deep relaxation and in helping you to focus on positive proactive thoughts and feelings, whilst leaving harmful negative thoughts and feelings behind. Having a few sessions of hypnotherapy prior to an important event could help you to focus on the occasion itself and on what you want to achieve without your focus straying into unhelpful thoughts of self-doubt.

Case Study:

Tabitha was a first year university student who was extremely anxious when we first met. She had always wanted to be a social worker. Working hard through her school and college years, she had been delighted to be accepted at one of the top universities for social work qualification. However, as the course progressed Tabitha became increasingly anxious about presenting her ideas in front of her seminar group and began to avoid some of her tutorials because of this. When she was informed that her assessment would require her to speak in front of her whole year group Tabitha felt over-whelmed. She began to believe that she would have to drop out of university and to give up her dream of becoming a social worker.

Over the following few weeks we were able to analyse what it was that made Tabitha feel she could not talk in public successfully. Tabitha remembered having to speak in front of her English class at school many years before. It had been an unsettling experience as she remembers stuttering a little when she began to speak and a couple of boys in the class began laughing at her. The teacher did not tackle their behaviour and other pupils began to giggle too. Tabitha began to blush and the whole experience became very upsetting. Tabitha remembers feeling very embarrassed and she was later teased by some of her class mates about her evident embarrassment. Understandably, Tabitha's first experience of public speaking had not felt positive and she had been left feeling silly, which had impacted negatively on her self-confidence. Following this experience, she would pretend to be ill in order to avoid school whenever she was required to speak in front of the class and was less likely to raise her hand to answer any of the teacher's questions.

Childhood experiences are often the cause of our lack of confidence and we spent some time looking at Tabitha's fear and the impact this had had on her when she was forced to speak in public. As we talked through the issue Tabitha began to realise that her audience at university were more mature and unlikely to be so rude and unkind as her young classmates had been.

We also began to think about how her fellow colleagues might feel about presenting their own work. Interestingly Tabitha stated, "Oh I know a couple of students who are dreading the presentation just like me".

We considered how Tabitha might work together with the other two students to build resilience and practice their presentations. On being approached, both students were very grateful for someone to work with and they were all able to support each other through the process. Tabitha was able to practice presenting and developing her presentation skills alongside the other students who gave support and useful feedback. As she began to relax a little and benefit from the support, Tabitha was able to focus on improving her delivery and the content of her presentation. Her self-confidence was growing and she was beginning to realise how capable she was.

Tabitha began to practice Mindfulness in order to manage her anxiety and downloaded a mobile phone app she could listen to whenever she felt stressed or anxious. This provided Tabitha with a reliable coping strategy and helped her to focus on her presentation and kept negative thoughts at bay. She was able to listen to a particularly relaxing Mindfulness track prior to presenting her final assessment and coped very well throughout the experience. I received a very excited text following that presentation. She understandably felt proud of her achievement. More importantly, she had been able to eradicate her *limiting belief* and could state "I can speak in public!"

Notes

Notes

Notes

Notes

Chapter Nine

The Power of Affirmations

Having a positive mental attitude is of great importance in building and maintaining confidence and promoting this attitude can be achieved and boosted by practising *affirmations*. An affirmation is a positive statement which when repeated can help us to re-programme our sub conscious thoughts. It can enable us to override negative and self-sabotaging thoughts and to remind ourselves of our attributes and strengths. These become positive truthful statements which when repeated, remind us of what we have to offer. Affirmations are best created by yourself but there are also apps available now which can assist you.

Studies in Cognitive Behavioural Therapy have taught us that when we think negatively about ourselves we tend to lower our mood and this has a damaging effect on our self-confidence. We are also aware that thinking positively about ourselves can have the opposite effect but it is not uncommon for us to fail to take this positive action. Practising to think positively about ourselves and our abilities can have a significant impact on the outcome of any event. Yet, it can be difficult to remember to think positively about ourselves at all times and it can be easy to fall back into bad habits. However, developing and practising affirmations routinely at certain times during the day (e.g. first thing in the morning whilst getting dressed) can ensure that we regularly give ourselves support and can help us to remain focused and empowered. Of course, thinking positively also helps to reduce stress.

It is believed that affirmations become more effective when spoken out loud and used at least daily, a number of times. Your affirmations of course will be personal and relevant to you and should be created to support you and remind you of your positive attributes or abilities. Here are a few examples:

Today will be a good day!

I am just as talented as any of my colleagues.

I WILL finish this work project today.

I am attractive in my own unique way.

I am likeable.

I CAN do well in this exam as I have worked hard for it.

I DO deserve this promotion.

If you were anxious about how you would cope on your first day in a new job, you might try saying the following affirmation five times before you arrive: *"I was chosen as the best candidate for the job and I will enjoy this role!"*

Or, if you were dreading seeing a difficult or challenging relative you might try the following affirmation: *"I CAN remain calm and just let their words wash over me".*

Remember to create an affirmation that is personal to you and contains the positive message that you need to hear to empower you.

Affirming your successes is hugely important in the maintenance of your confidence. Always ensure you celebrate each success, no matter how small, as your confidence will be maintained and sustained.

"I got the job! There were 200 candidates, I must have impressed them because THEY chose ME!!"

Case Study:

I met Melissa a few years ago when she had just become a newly qualified teacher and she came to see me having secured her first full-time teaching post in a local primary school. Melissa was extremely anxious and this was having an impact on her confidence.

Melissa had always lacked self-confidence despite passing her teaching qualifications with flying colours and she was struggling with what is often described as *imposter syndrome.* This is the consistent inability to believe that one's achievements or successes are legitimately due to one's own efforts or abilities. Imposter syndrome is common amongst people with low self-confidence and sadly successes are often put down to *luck* and the benefits of success are not enjoyed. Indeed, if you feel landing a new job was due to some lucky occurrence rather than your own abilities, you are likely to worry about keeping that job long-term.

Melissa was in her first two weeks of teaching a Year Two class and felt comfortable with the children and her role.

All the teaching staff had been welcoming and friendly towards Melissa but she still felt terrified when attending staff meetings and especially during the lunchbreak when she was expected to eat her lunch in the staff room. Melissa felt very self-conscious and had found a number of excuses to avoid entering the staff room. She told me, "I just feel like a fraud and that if I chat to the other teachers, they may realise that I'm not as good a teacher. What if they think I am useless?"

Melissa and I spent a little while understanding and rationalising her feelings and her lack of self-confidence, being so new to her first full time teaching role. After some analysis and discussion, together we determined a number of facts about the situation:

- Melissa is a newly qualified teacher.
- This is Melissa's first teaching role.
- Melissa has been selected from a list of other candidates because she clearly demonstrated promise and the interview panel had liked what she had had to say in the interview.

Melissa agreed that these statements were indeed factual, furthermore, we went on to agree further facts:

- Melissa's colleagues knew that she was a newly qualified teacher in her first full time teaching role.
- Melissa's colleagues had been newly qualified themselves in the past and therefore understood that your first teaching post can be challenging initially and they would not expect her to know as much about teaching as an experienced teacher.

- Melissa's colleagues knew that she had been selected from a number of equally qualified candidates because of her achievements and because she was deemed the best candidate for the role.

Melissa understood that all of the above facts were true but she still struggled to ignore her self-sabotaging thoughts. We worked together on developing some affirmations and Melissa agreed to read them out every morning before she went to work. She also decided to do this standing in front of her mirror with outstretched arms (something a friend suggested to her having found it had helped them in the past). These were the affirmations Melissa developed:

I am a good teacher and I gained my qualification with good grades.

I am great with children.

I was chosen for this role as I was considered the best candidate for the job.

My colleagues have been welcoming and they all understand I am new to this role.

Melissa repeated her affirmations every day, three times each before work, and she emailed me with an update on her progress two weeks later stating "I don't know how it works Anne, but the affirmations we created are really making a difference! I have found that saying them out loud to my smiling reflection in the mirror also helps. I somehow feel stronger and more confident, and I know the affirmations are true so I can relax more about everything. I plan to continue using affirmations because they definitely set a positive tone for the day."

I receive lots of emails like the one Melissa sent me about the power of affirmations. I think this is because my clients are so surprised that something so simple can be so effective. Not only do positive affirmations help to reprogramme your thought processes they are equally important in helping to keep negative thoughts at bay. Whilst you are working on thinking positively, you are no longer focussing on negative self-sabotaging thoughts. Positive affirmations divert you and protect you from their powerful damaging effects.

Exercise

What self-sabotaging thoughts do you have about yourself? How have these negative thoughts impacted on you in the past? Now try writing some positive affirmations that can support and empower you in the future. Be your own cheerleader, focus on your positive attributes and strengths.

Begin by affirming all your past achievements and then develop some affirmations that you can repeat daily to build or maintain your confidence. There are some examples below:

I am good at my job.

People like me.

I try hard and I do my best.

_____

_____

_____

_____
_____
_____
_____
_____
_____
_____
_____
_____
_____
_____
_____
_____
_____

Notes

Notes

Notes

Chapter Ten

Socialising, Dating and Networking

The majority of the clients I work with struggle to socialise due to their lack of self-confidence. Many can confidently carry out their work roles or mix with old friends and feel comfortable doing so. However, it is the thought of meeting new people and of how they might be perceived or interpreted that worries them most.

Exercise

Below are some of the fears and feelings that have been expressed by attendees during workshops. Tick those that you feel *you* may have experienced yourself in the past when you have attended social events.

What can I wear that will make me feel slimmer, taller, more professional, etc?

How will I cope if I get lost on the way and arrive late?

How will I cope if everyone stares at me when I first walk in?

How will I cope if they don't like me?

How will I cope if I am left on my own with no one to talk to?

How will I cope if I am expected to talk about myself... what can I say?

How will I cope if I don't know anyone there?

How will I cope if I don't like anyone there?

How will I cope if someone says something rude to me?

How will I cope if I try to speak but my mouth goes dry and I don't know what to say?

How will I cope if it is really boring?

How will I cope if they are talking about something I don't understand or know anything about? How can I join in?

How will I cope if I am expected to dance?

How will I cope if they can tell that I am shy or anxious?

How will I cope if I don't get a second date?

These are just a small sample of the types of fears I come across throughout my work but there are many many more. One of my clients had Alopecia and they focussed all their anxieties around this. What if they notice my bald spot? What if they ask me about it? How will I feel? How will I cover my embarrassment?

In social situations we usually want to make a great impression and to be liked or appreciated. This can place us under great pressure which can result in experiencing social anxiety.

Seeing the Bigger Picture

I have worked with people from all walks of life who struggle with social anxiety and it is more common than you might think! In just one month I have worked with an accounts clerk who avoids office parties, a teacher who struggles to talk to colleagues in the staff room, a model who feels self-conscious about her height at parties, a mum who avoids chatting with other mums at the school gates and even a managing director who fears talking to staff in the canteen. When we are anxious prior to a first date or social engagement, we rarely think about how nervous other people at the event may also be feeling. My work reminds me of this almost every day. At any party, it is believed that at least 50% of guests experience some anxiety. Of course, once the wine begins to flow, most will get over their nerves very quickly. Experiencing fear prior to the event can often put us off going altogether. However, knowing that we are not alone is the first step in overcoming social anxiety and in building our self-confidence in social settings.

Cracking Communication

So how can we manage anxiety in social settings and begin to relish and enjoy these occasions. Learning how to communicate effectively is the key to enabling yourself to meet new people, make new friends or simply get along with colleagues. The case below typifies many of the experiences I hear about from those who attend my workshops and I have provided some strategies and solutions throughout which might prove useful to you also.

Case Study: Becky

Becky is 24 and she works for a busy marketing company. Since working for the company, she had lost touch with many of her old school and college friends and her social life had become almost non-existent. She stated that she would love to have a relationship but did not know how and when she might meet someone new. She often received invitations on evenings out to pubs or restaurants but had been avoiding these social occasions for some time. She told me that although she would love to be involved, she could not manage the fear and anxiety she felt before and during such events. She also feared that eventually colleagues would stop asking her to these events because of her constant refusals.

The main fears she expressed were:

1. *Walking into the room for the first time.* This is when most people will look up and greet you and may even compliment you on your appearance. For people who lack self-confidence, this can be the most difficult part of socialising and they can be left feeling embarrassed and self-conscious.

2. *Striking up that first conversation with someone you do not really know:* When you feel anxious or fearful, small talk can be difficult to achieve. Becky stated that her mind often goes blank, her mouth goes dry and she can't think of what to say. Others tell me that they can sometimes talk too much, not allowing others to speak, for fear of there being a long embarrassing silence.

3. *Keeping the conversation going and knowing when to move on and chat to someone new:* For someone like Becky, the thought of having a long conversation with someone they may not know can be terrifying. Many self-conscious people worry about what to say and how they will be perceived by others. Also, it is a good thing to move around and 'mingle' at social events but many feel anxious about how to move on politely and whether they will appear rude.

4. *How to take friendships to the next level:* Becky tells me that she has met some lovely people in the past but does not know how to develop these budding friendships or potential relationships. Knowing when and how to build new connections is key in developing our social network or in finding a partner.

5. *How to retain friends and maintain an active social life:* Once you build a good social network, it is important to put some effort into maintaining this. It is often tempting to let others invite you to social engagements as it can make you feel 'wanted'. However, to maintain a good social network, you need to do some of the organising and inviting yourself. Those that do all the work often don't feel valued and this is not a great state of affairs if you want to retain friendships.

6. *Dating and how to overcome low self-confidence:* You can feel vulnerable when you enter the 'dating game'. However, you *can* manage your anxieties and gently push yourself out of your comfort zone in order to build relationships. Understanding some of the rules of engagement, can help you to build resilience and find the perfect partner.

Becky and I began to work on strategies to help her to manage her concerns so that she could begin saying 'Yes' to future invitations.

1. *Walking into the room for the first time.*

    Becky was very self-conscious about her appearance. Despite being an attractive young woman, she focussed on imperfections she perceived about herself and these negative perceptions had continued to lower her self-confidence over the years. My experience tells me that many of my clients see things they would like to change about their appearance yet these tiny imperfections often go unnoticed by others. No one is completely perfect, indeed what is perfection? Every person's perception is different. I asked Becky to think of five people she would consider could walk into a room at a party feeling confident. The conversation went something like this:

    "Becky, can you think of five people you know who might walk into the room at a party and could feel self-confident?"

    "Yes – Mark, Sarah, Michelle, Erin and Phil (her work colleagues)".

    "Can you tell me any imperfections they have in their physical appearance?"

    "Erm, no! They are all very attractive in their own way".

    "Nothing? Can you imagine that they could all become fashion models if they wanted to change their careers one day?"

    This made Becky laugh initially. "Oh no, not at all".

"Why not?"

"Okay. I understand your point. We all have some imperfections!"

Once we established that no one is completely perfect (because we don't know what perfection really is), we were able to make some progress. Becky understood that everyone she knew presented themselves in the best way they could and made the most of their best features, just like Becky did. She realised that she did not see imperfections in others because she liked or admired them for who they were and not, how they looked. We began to develop a few strategies that Becky could use to manage her anxieties about entering a room. Becky found that listening to a Mindfulness track on her phone before she arrived helped her to calm down a little. Sometimes you can arrange to collect someone on the way to a party and then you could arrive together. Another strategy would be to focus on one person who you know you can talk to easily as you enter the room, and make your way over to them immediately to open a conversation or to say hello. You might then avoid looking around to see who else has arrived until you feel a little more relaxed.

2. *Striking up that first conversation with someone you do not really know.*

Social conversations can be a great deal easier than you think. They often follow a similar pattern and you can learn how to strike up a conversation with anyone if you learn a few conversational techniques. You might open a conversation with someone you don't know by smiling and asking an opening question.

"So how long have you known Sara? How did you get here tonight?" Or, "so do you know a lot of people here tonight?" Once they answer, you can introduce yourself. "I'm Becky by the way".

Most social conversations begin in this simple way and can continue comfortably by asking some *Open Questions*. These are the questions which require more of an explanation rather than a simple 'yes' or 'no' answer and they help to get conversations flowing. Most common ones are, "what do you do?" or, "so what is it like working at Smiths?". These are the initial questions that get people talking about themselves and as they relax and share thoughts or stories with you it can help you to relax and answer the inevitable questions that will follow about yourself.

Becky and I worked on conversational techniques together and she practised how she might begin a conversation. She also considered beforehand how she might talk about herself, and what others might find interesting to hear. People generally like talking about themselves, so if you keep asking questions, the conversation should flow.

3. *Keeping the conversation going and knowing when to move on and chat to someone new at large gatherings.*

If you feel that the conversation is becoming a little more difficult and you do not feel you have a lot in common with the person you are chatting to, you might want to 'move on'. If you are in a group, that is fairly easy as you can bring someone else into the conversation without leaving the first person out.

"So do you work at the same company as Kelly?" However, you can simply excuse yourself to get a drink or go to the toilet and try to engage someone else on the way back. In the meantime the first person will have usually begun to chat to someone else. You can also say, "It's been lovely chatting to you," as you go which signifies that the conversation may not continue. This was particularly difficult for Becky and we worked on this for a little while. However, it is worth knowing that this is something that most people struggle with but it's an essential part of socialising and must happen in order to meet new people.

4. *How to take friendships to the next level*

Like many people, Becky was always anxious about how to develop friendships. She had allowed others to invite her to social occasions as this reassured her that she was liked by them. However, she had been too frightened in the past to reciprocate or arrange an evening out for colleagues for fear of rejection.

Once Becky began to attend a few social engagements, we considered if she had any common interests with her colleagues. She discovered that Clare in the office next door wanted to join a gym but hadn't done a great deal about it. Becky also wanted to join a gym and had mentioned this the last time they had chatted but neither took any action. We considered how this might be resolved and Becky agreed to email Clare. She stated that she had noticed that the local gym were promoting some introductory offers, and she asked Clare if she would like to join herself in attending an 'open evening'.

Emailing Clare felt less stressful for Becky than inviting Clare in person. We had discussed the possible outcome beforehand. This might be just the opportunity Clare had been waiting for to take some action concerning her fitness. However, Clare might not be available on Thursday. Also joining a gym can feel like a big commitment so if Clare opted not to attend, Becky could be understanding about this. She could also promise to let her know what the new gym was like in case she changed her mind in the future.

It can take a little courage to invite others out socially and we have to accept that the answer will never be 'Yes' every time. The important thing is to keep trying as success *will* follow at some point.

5.   *How to retain friends and maintain an active social life:*

Everyone wants to feel important and wanted! This is the most important thing to remember in maintaining friendships. If you allow others to always invite you along to social engagements and never reciprocate, they may feel taken for granted at some point. Try to remember that each and every one of us all need to feel important to others. You may not feel confident enough to throw a party, but you can invite others for a coffee or to watch a film. Remember that they have wanted your company at events in the past and have invited you along so there is every reason to believe that they will welcome your invitation.

Try to schedule regular invites once a month or so and if friends cannot attend, make sure you ask them again soon. I send out a group text every month or so to my girlfriends to ask about their availability and suggest an activity. *"Happy hour at the Cocktail Bar girls? When would you all be free?"*. By communicating in this way, everyone knows this is a group event and it's easy to co-ordinate diaries.

If you feel one of your friends is having a difficult time, ask to meet them for coffee and show support.

6. *Dating and how to overcome low self-confidence:*

Whether you meet someone through your work on a night out or via the internet, dating can be nerve-wracking for those who lack confidence. If you are interested in someone, get to know more about them first. Find out a little more about their hobbies or work and show a genuine interest. If you feel there is perhaps a spark, show some interest in the next football match or suggest you might support them at their next gig. Gauge their response and take it from there!

Internet dating has its pitfalls but can be a great way of meeting a new partner. You are able to learn a little more about the individual and get to know them by chatting on the phone initially before braving a first date. However, many of my clients struggle to write an online profile about themselves. They do not want to describe themselves as 'attractive' for example, in case they are perceived as boastful or arrogant. Nonetheless, it is very important to describe yourself honestly, if you are to meet the right person. Why not ask a friend to write the profile for you? Becky asked her sister to help out with her dating profile and it read:

My sister Becky is attractive, funny and kind hearted. She is not the type to write a dating profile about herself easily as she is also very modest! Becky is very outgoing once she gets to know you and is great company. She enjoys eating out and weekends away and is an accomplished snow boarder... (you get the idea).

You could however begin your profile with something like *My friends would describe me as kind and a bit zany...* Whichever way you choose to describe who you are, just remember that this is all the reader knows about you initially, so you have to express yourself fully. Be positive and focus on your good points – no one needs to know you are grumpy at times – we all are!

Of course you may wish to add a photograph to your online profile. If you do, remember that a picture can paint a thousand words! Be aware that you only get one chance to make a first impression, ensure that your photograph is a recent one and reflects your personality. Note that the person who views your profile is trying to get an indication of the type of person you are and your hobbies and interests so being pictured in a pub with a pint of beer in your hand may imply you may spend too much time there.

Most people would feel a little nervous before a date. You need to remind yourself that not every date will result in meeting the partner of your dreams, you may need to kiss a few frogs before you meet your prince or princess charming. Allow yourself just to see what happens and take pressure off yourself. If the other person does not want a second date, then they were not the right person for you! Dating is a bit like interviewing... You cannot employ every candidate.

Notes

Notes

Notes

Chapter Eleven

Maintaining Your Confidence and Becoming Resilient

Once you have found your true confident self, it is important to hang on to it!! We all know that the trials and tribulations of life can have an impact on our confidence and it is important to learn the skills you need to maintain the confidence you feel and the progress you have made. Being resilient is about recovering from setbacks in the minimum of time and feeling able to adapt to change. The longer we focus upon the negative things that happen to us, the more we lower our mood and damage our self-confidence. For some, failing an exam or getting through the interview process for a dream job can set our confidence back for months or years. But for resilient people, such setbacks will not stop them from achieving all they set out to achieve.

Maintaining a Logical Stance

It's easy to see how failing an exam might make you feel that the qualification is perhaps too difficult for you. However, this is usually because we focus on what failure means at that moment in time. It may prevent you from attending the university you wanted, or prevent you from setting out on your chosen profession. But this is a *temporary* state of affairs and does not mean you cannot achieve in the end. Remember that failure is often just one of the necessary stages along the road to success. Many students fail to get high enough grades to go to their chosen university – it is extremely common. Some have to accept their second choice but the initial disappointment fades in a short time and it results in them loving where they eventually study. Others, focussed on their dream, choose to re-sit their exams. Those that do, enter the re-sits far more knowledgeable about the course and are clearer about those areas they need to focus upon and therefore get better results second time around.

Have you ever attended an interview for your ideal job, working so hard on the interview presentation, and then felt devastated when you didn't get that job offer? Well with the average job attracting between 40 – 700 applicants, job applications can be challenging. If you get to the shortlist or interview stage however, this tells you that you have in fact done extremely well and is an indication that you will find a great job before too long. It is important at this point to ask for some feedback from the company in order to make the experience a useful learning opportunity so that you can embark on the next application better prepared. If you focus on the result too long however, you may lower your mood and motivation and cease applying for other roles. Allow yourself to wallow in your disappointment for no more than an hour, and then focus on the next step to getting what it is that you want.

Practical steps you can take to maintain self-confidence

Having developed your self-confidence, there are a number of things you can do to retain it for years to come:

- *Take care of yourself:* By eating healthily and getting regular exercise, we feel fitter and stronger. This raises our Serotonin levels in the body which helps us to feel more positive. This may also have the added benefit of improving the way we look too! Taking our physical welfare seriously is important if we are to continue to feel good about ourselves.

- *Get plenty of sleep:* If we do not get the amount or quality of sleep that we need (usually considered to be around eight hours), this will eventually have an impact on our mood and our overall health. To retain a positive outlook, feeling fresh and well rested is vital. Take steps to improve your sleep where necessary by taking the time out to achieve the required hours and ensuring your bedroom is a restful place, free from mobile phones and other distractions.

- *Make the most of leisure time:* Having interests and seeing friends or family is important in maintaining good mental health. If we can achieve a good work-life balance, having things to look forward to in the evenings or at weekends, we keep our self-confidence and feel more buoyant. Spending time on activities that we enjoy and having a variety of experiences or conversations with a large social network reinforces our self-confidence and helps us to feel good about ourselves. Join a club, see an old friend or go for a long walk and discover a new place… it all helps.

- *Keep anxiety at bay:* It is very important that we manage any anxiety that occurs without allowing it to develop. Anxious thoughts can lead to self-doubt so don't give them house room! Use the relaxation tips listed earlier in the book, or find something else that works for you, and practise this regularly. Anxiety is a normal human experience and we can accept this and manage it accordingly so that it never damages our self-confidence.

- *Refresh your new skills regularly:* If you overcome your fear of public speaking or have been practising assertiveness with success, maintain and develop these achievements over time. By continuing to be assertive with others or speaking regularly in meetings we maintain our skills and our self-confidence. Continue to take yourself slightly out of your comfort zone. Each time we use our new skills we reinforce our self-confidence and remind ourselves how confident we really are.

- *Avoid 'Confidence Crushers':* Continue to avoid those situations and people who drain you of energy and self-confidence. Retain a strong network of supportive friends, family members and colleagues who sustain you and ensure you offer them similar support. Being able to share your fears with someone who can remind you of how capable you are is very powerful.

- *Be your best supporter:* Retaining a positive inner voice over time is one of the most important things you can do to maintain your confidence. Allow yourself to make mistakes occasionally and be sure to remember all the great things that you have achieved when this occurs. Being self-critical just lowers your mood further and applies extra pressure. Being kind to yourself and using encouraging self-talk can help you to bounce back from a disappointment and to focus on the next step.

Authors note

My experience of working with others to develop their self-confidence has taught me a great deal about people. Most want to achieve success in some way and a lack of self-confidence prevents them from doing so. My older clients wish they had tackled the problem earlier and enjoyed their lives more and the younger one's fear missing out on something. Self-confidence really is the key to doing, and potentially having more.

A number of research projects have demonstrated that it is the confident people who succeed in life, over and above those who have the knowledge and skills but choose not to use them. I hope you have enjoyed reading this book but more importantly, I hope it has motivated you to take action.

My experience of working with confident people tells me they are more successful and happier people. Furthermore, happier in their own skin, they seem to want to share what they have with others. Enjoy it!

Notes

Notes

Notes

Coaching others to achieve self-confidence has become my life's work and I am always interested to hear from readers about their experiences and their own confidence building strategies. If you would like to share your experiences from your 'Confidence Journey', I would love to hear from you!!

Anne Millne-Riley

www.confidenceguru.com

Bibliography

[1] Waite, M. and Hawker, S. (2009) *Oxford Dictionary and Thesaurus*, Oxford, Oxford University Press, P.184

[2] *The Readers Digest Universal Dictionary*, (1988) Turnhout, Belgium, The Readers Digest Association Limited, P.334

[3] Ford, H. (2009) *My Life and Work*, London, BN Publishing

[4] Heppell, M, (2011) *Flip-It – How to get the best out of everything*, London, Pearson Life

[5] Miller, A., Doran, C., Cunningham, J. (1981) Article in *Management Review*, 'There's a smart way to write management goals and objectives'

[6] Popular quote attributed to Thomas Edison, American Inventor, 1847–1931

[7] Ford, H. in collaboration with Crowther, S. (1922) *My Life and Work*, New York, Garden City Publishing Company

[8] This popular quote is widely attributed to Vince Lombardi, American Football Coach, (1913–70)

[9] Another popular quote widely attributed to F. Scott Fitzgerald, Writer, 1896-1940.

[10] Popular quote attributed to Thomas A. Edison, American Inventor, 1847-1931

[11] Popular quote attributed to Truman Capote, American Novelist, 1924-1984

[12] Richard Branson quote accessed via his Virgin Website (13/10/18) https://www.virgin.com/richard-branson/you-learn-doing-and-falling-over

Lightning Source UK Ltd.
Milton Keynes UK
UKHW041816050219
336792UK00001B/71/P